THE ARCHITECTURE LOVER'S GUIDE TO
ROME

When I was in my second year of art school, I had an art history professor whose method of teaching changed my way of thinking about art and architecture. Rather than just have us memorise names and dates and genres, he presented the arts in their historical context, and described how they were influenced by and reflective of contemporary events. In my mind, it was as though someone had turned on a light to illuminate the past. His lectures were engaging and insightful, and his enthusiasm for the material was infectious. Later in life, I was honoured (and still a little star-struck) to count him as a friend and colleague. He died too young, and with plenty still left to teach.

Thank you, Kevin Dean, for turning on the light.

THE ARCHITECTURE LOVER'S GUIDE TO
ROME

ELIZABETH F. HEATH

WHITE OWL

AN IMPRINT OF PEN & SWORD BOOKS LTD.
YORKSHIRE – PHILADELPHIA

First published in Great Britain in 2019 by
PEN & SWORD WHITE OWL
An imprint of
Pen & Sword Books Ltd
Yorkshire - Philadelphia

ISBN 9781526735799

Printed and bound by Replika Press Pvt. Ltd.
Design: Paul Wilkinson.

Cartographer: Liz Puhl
Research Assistant: Suzie Dundas

Pen & Sword Books Limited incorporates the imprints
of Atlas, Archaeology, Aviation, Discovery, Family
History, Fiction, History, Maritime, Military, Military
Classics, Politics, Select, Transport, True Crime, Air
World, Frontline Publishing, Leo Cooper, Remember
When, Seaforth Publishing, The Praetorian Press,
Wharncliffe Local History, Wharncliffe Transport,
Wharncliffe True Crime and White Owl.

For a complete list of Pen & Sword titles please contact
PEN & SWORD BOOKS LIMITED
47 Church Street, Barnsley, South Yorkshire, S70 2AS,
United Kingdom
E-mail: enquiries@pen-and-sword.co.uk
Website: www.pen-and-sword.co.uk

Or
PEN AND SWORD BOOKS
1950 Lawrence Rd, Havertown, PA 19083, USA
E-mail: Uspen-and-sword@casematepublishers.com
Website: www.penandswordbooks.com

CONTENTS

THE PORTICO OF OCTAVIA AS PARABLE
Architecture and Complexity in Rome

THIS IS THE *Porticus Otaviae*, the *Portico d'Ottavia* or the Portico of Octavia, located in the heart of Rome's *centro storico*, the historic centre. In Roman architecture, a portico, also called a pronaos, is essentially a much more elaborate version of what we think of as a porch. This was a monumental covered entryway, or *propylaeum*, that formed the entrance to a temple complex. It was the focal point of a colonnaded walkway that formed a perimeter around the temples of Jupiter Stator and Juno Regina. The illustration below, from a 1911 book on the monuments of Rome, shows how the portico probably looked during its apex.

The first image, of the present-day portico, is one of my favourites in this guidebook. Not because it's a particularly stunning photograph, but because it sums up the complicated nature of Rome's architectural history, and the challenge of trying to sort it all out into some kind of chronological timeline. Consider what we know about the phases of construction, additions and repairs, and the uses of the portico area:

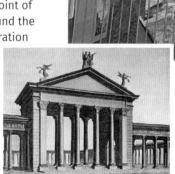

Reconstruction of the Portico as it once was.
Image from S.B. Platner, The Topography and Monuments of Ancient Rome (2nd ed.), p. 372, 1911.

The Portico d' Ottavia today.

- The temples the portico encloses were constructed in the second century, BCE.
- The portico itself was constructed more than 150 years later, on orders of Emperor Augustus, in honour of his sister, Ottavia (Octavia) Minor.
- On at least two occasions in the first century CE, the structure was badly damaged by fire and restored.
- In 442 CE, an earthquake levelled the two right-hand columns, which were replaced with the brick archway still visible today.

- By the early Middle Ages, a fish market was established on the ruins of the portico.

- In 772, the church of Sant'Angelo in Pescheria (*pescheria* refers to the fish market) was built over the original temples. The stairs and green door at the back of the portico belong to the church, and three columns from the portico were incorporated into the left-hand side of the church façade.

- In 1555, Pope Paul IV ordered that all of the city's Jewish population be forcibly moved into an area of a few square blocks adjacent to the portico. The area, which became known as the Ghetto of Rome, was walled-in and had four gates, which were locked shut at night. One gate was to the left of the Portico of Octavia. The Ghetto was an unsanitary, overcrowded neighbourhood subject to frequent flooding and outbreaks of disease. Residents were only allowed to leave the Ghetto during daylight hours, and they had to be back inside the walls by sundown.

- In the late 1700s, Jews from the Ghetto were forced to attend Jesuit sermons every Saturday, delivered in the ruins of the Portico of Octavia, which also remained a fish market well into the 1800s.

- With the establishment of the Kingdom of Italy in 1870, the Ghetto was abolished. In 1888 the Ghetto walls were torn down. In 1943, the Nazis occupied Rome, and sent more than 1,000 of its Jewish residents to death camps. A plaque near the portico remembers those who were sent away and never returned.

- Today, the Portico of Octavia flanks the eastern entrance to the area still referred to as the Ghetto. Romans and tourists alike visit here today, to look for traces of its past as a Jewish enclave and to eat in one of the many restaurants along Via del Portico d'Ottavia, where Roman-Jewish cuisine is the specialty.

A first-century BCE monument, built over second-century temples, with fifth-century restorations and an eighth-century

church growing out of its ruins. A bustling marketplace and a symbol of religious prosecution. A tourist attraction and a place of remembrance.

Welcome to Rome!

The Portico of Octavia serves as a fitting example of how architecture has evolved organically in a city that's been continuously occupied for nearly 3,000 years. Rome has never been frozen in time – it's been an evolving, constantly changing city since its inception. It's never completely intact and it's rarely pristine – even buildings like the Pantheon and St Peter's Basilica, both models for their architectural styles and periods, differ significantly from their original designs. Instead, the architecture of Rome is the stage set on which a dynamic, living city goes about its daily business. It's at turns soaring and inspirational, crumbling and chaotic, functional and severe. It's been pillaged and preserved, restored and bastardised. Its most revered monuments, before they were elevated to their current iconic status, were once cattle pastures, marble quarries and yes, fish markets.

So, how can a casual guidebook on the architecture of Rome sort out this complicated chronology and overlapping layers of styles, periods and modifications? To do so comprehensively would take years of research, and result in a voluminous academic tome instead of an accessible, portable guidebook. Instead, this guide uses some of Rome's key buildings and monuments as examples of the major styles and phases of architecture that have risen in the city over its long history. It offers a 'greatest hits' timeline – as well as some worthy B-sides – that demonstrate the practical, political and spiritual uses of architecture in Rome, what each building represented at its zenith, and what each has come to represent since. Instead of a complete guide to the Roman Forum or a directory of every important church, I've chosen to highlight specific buildings that exemplify a style or time period. In doing so, I hope to provide some context and subtext for readers fascinated by the architecture of the Eternal City and hoping to make at least a little sense of it all.

A note on how to use this guidebook

Since there's nothing linear about the architectural history of Rome, it's likewise impossible for a tour of Rome's architectural highlights to proceed in any kind of a straight line. This map of central Rome includes all of the buildings and monuments covered in this guide (with a few exceptions that are outside the centre and so noted on the map). Fortunately for travellers, Rome has a compact, flat city centre, and most of the sights included in this guide can be reached on foot.

Throughout the guide, I've included information on opening hours and admission fees if applicable, best times to visit, and directives for using public transportation. Please keep in mind that things like opening hours and bus routes are about the only things that change quickly in Rome, so please confirm before you set out.

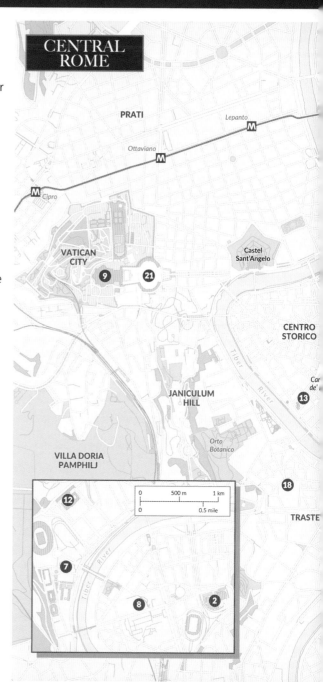

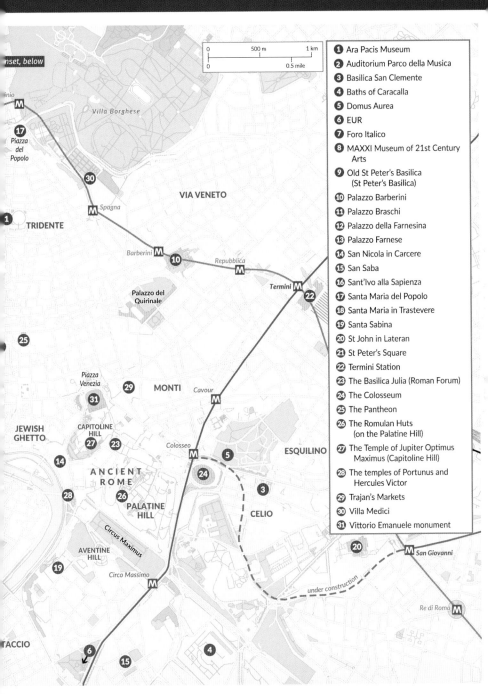

1. Ara Pacis Museum
2. Auditorium Parco della Musica
3. Basilica San Clemente
4. Baths of Caracalla
5. Domus Aurea
6. EUR
7. Foro Italico
8. MAXXI Museum of 21st Century Arts
9. Old St Peter's Basilica (St Peter's Basilica)
10. Palazzo Barberini
11. Palazzo Braschi
12. Palazzo della Farnesina
13. Palazzo Farnese
14. San Nicola in Carcere
15. San Saba
16. Sant'Ivo alla Sapienza
17. Santa Maria del Popolo
18. Santa Maria in Trastevere
19. Santa Sabina
20. St John in Lateran
21. St Peter's Square
22. Termini Station
23. The Basilica Julia (Roman Forum)
24. The Colosseum
25. The Pantheon
26. The Romulan Huts (on the Palatine Hill)
27. The Temple of Jupiter Optimus Maximus (Capitoline Hill)
28. The temples of Portunus and Hercules Victor
29. Trajan's Markets
30. Villa Medici
31. Vittorio Emanuele monument

0   500 m   1 km
0   0.5 mile

inset, below

Villa Borghese

17 Piazza del Popolo

30

VIA VENETO

Spagna

1 TRIDENTE

Barberini

10

Repubblica

Termini 22

Palazzo del Quirinale

25

Piazza Venezia

31

29 MONTI

Cavour

JEWISH GHETTO

CAPITOLINE HILL

27 23

Colosseo

ESQUILINO

14

ANCIENT ROME

5

3

28

26

PALATINE HILL

CELIO

Circus Maximus

AVENTINE HILL

20

San Giovanni

19

Circo Massimo

TACCIO

under construction

Re di Roma

6

4

15

1

ROMULUS PUTS DOWN ROOTS

The Palatine Hill and the Romulan Hut

The origins of Rome are a blend in equal parts of legend, hypothesis and verifiable evidence. The architecture of Rome, along with first-person accounts written by the likes of Julius Caesar, Augustus, Livy and Plutarch, is perhaps the most essential aspect of that verifiable evidence.

The legend is that twin brothers Romulus and Remus, abandoned as infants and suckled by a she-wolf, were the children of Rhea Silvia, a vestal virgin seduced by Mars, the god of war. When, as adults, the twins quarrelled about where to found a new settlement and who would lead it, Romulus killed his brother. On 21 April 753 BCE, he is said to have founded his new city on the Palatine Hill, named it after himself and made himself its first king. He is credited with creating the Senate, establishing military and religious customs and a pantheon of gods, and codifying Rome's earliest laws regarding property, civil rights and citizenship. Some fifty years into his rule, he is said to have disappeared in the midst of a storm, only to be installed on Mount Olympus as the god Quirinus.

As Rome transformed from primitive riverine settlement to an organised republic and, centuries later, an empire, this foundation myth endured and was enhanced. By the first century BCE, Virgil, at the behest of Emperor Augustus, nephew and adopted son of Julius Caesar, had penned his epic poem, *The Aeneid*. It traced the journey of Aeneas, one of a handful of survivors of the Sack of Troy, from the near east to Carthage and Sicily and eventually, to the Italian peninsula. Virgil's epic firmly affixed Aeneas as the heroic forbearer of the Roman people.

The Aeneid also established a direct bloodline from Aeneas to Rhea Silvia. Because Aeneas was the son of Venus (the Roman version of the Greek Aphrodite), his progeny, including Romulus and Remus, were therefore of divine origin, as were the emperors of the Julian family, including Julius Caesar

An Iron Age funerary urn suggests the likely shape of the Romulan Hut. Walters Art Museum.

scholars believe that Romulus and Remus were not actual historical figures, but an amalgam of several Greek and Latin legendary and real characters. They theorise that even the name 'Romulus' was created retroactively to support the foundation myth as it was codified into Roman history.

The verifiable evidence is where architecture comes in. The Palatine Hill is home to one of the oldest archaeological remains in Rome, the so-called Romulan Hut, or *Casa Romuli*. This Iron Age (900–700 BCE) hut was made of wattle and daub, with a straw roof, a small awning and an animal-skin flap at the doorway. All that remains today are the postholes, which confirm its circular shape. During a 2006 excavation in the Roman Forum, tombs were found containing hut-shaped funerary urns. These dated to the same period and culture as the hut remains on the Palatine. Since it was customary for the ashes of the dead to be housed in clay urns that mimicked the shape of their dwellings, the urns further corroborate the style of the hut.

The site of the Romulan Hut was a place of reverence in Republican Rome, and it was maintained and restored through the Late Republican era. The Palatine Hill became the site of Imperial residences; Augustus symbolically chose a location adjacent to the Romulan Hut to build his palace, large parts of which are still extant today.

Modern visitors to the Palatine Hill can visit the Romulan Hut (*Casa Romuli*),

and Augustus. Romulus himself was deified after his death; 21 April is still celebrated as the anniversary of the founding of Rome.

The accepted hypothesis is that sometime in the eighth or ninth century BCE, a permanent settlement was established on the Palatine Hill, which was bordered on one side by the Tiber River and on the other by a swampy valley – the area that would become the Roman Forum. Other Latin tribes built similar, simple pastoral communities on neighbouring hills; eventually these were absorbed, either organically or by force, into the city that would grow into the Roman Republic.

The authenticity of Romulus as a historical figure is far less widely accepted. For the most part, Classical

but some imagination is needed to envision what it once looked like. A cluster of postholes – the impressions left where wooden posts, since deteriorated, once held up the roof – are etched into the *tufa* bedrock that forms much of the Palatine. Crisscrossing these scant remains are Republican- and Imperial-era foundation walls and haphazardly placed marble fragments.

While the name *Casa Romuli* takes some creative license, the term correctly links the remains to the approximate era of the Romulus and the founding of Rome in the eighth century BCE. Still, the presence of the hut remains does not confirm a solid date, prove Rome's foundation myth or verify the existence of Romulus; it only provides evidence that at least as early as 800–701 BCE – and possibly several hundred years earlier than that – a permanent settlement existed on the Palatine.

Unlike the largely accepted consensus

Postholes and foundation floor of the Casa Romuli, with later walls and foundations built on top.
Vitold Muratov/Wikimedia Commons.

reached among academics concerning the Romulan Hut, interpretation of a 1988 excavation has generated controversy and a fair amount of scepticism. During a multi-year excavation on the north-eastern slope of the Palatine Hill, an archaeological team unearthed a wall built from red tufa blocks. It fronted a large, natural gully that had been made steeper as a result of human excavations – typical of early defensive walls. Pottery sherds and other physical evidence date the wall to at least the seventh century BCE, and possibly earlier.

Ancient Roman historian Livy wrote that: 'Romulus's first act was to fortify the Palatine, the scene of his upbringing.' Other ancient sources also claim that Romulus ordered the wall built as his first step in establishing his settlement.

Some scholars have pointed to Livy, Virgil and other sources of the foundation myth, together with the discovery of the wall, to claim that the discovery was of a specific moment in ancient history – when Romulus drew the boundary of his new city and ordered that a wall be built to defend it. This theory supports the 'historicity,' or actual existence of Romulus. Critics of the thesis argue that science cannot use ancient literature to prove the origins of the wall, and in turn use the wall to prove the veracity of the ancient literature – and that of Romulus himself.

Still, like the Romulan Hut, the Palatine Wall, which can today be seen

HOW TO SEE IT: To see the remains of the Casa Romuli, visit the Palatine Hill archaeological area. A combined ticket includes admission to the Palatine, the Colosseum and the Roman Forum. The site opens at 8.30 am and remains open until 4.30 or 5 pm during winter months, and until 7.15 pm during peak summer season. Check https://www.coopculture.it/en/heritage.cfm?id=4 for current information. Also look for information about a S.U.P.E.R. Ticket, which includes admission to the houses of Livia and Augustus and other sites otherwise inaccessible. Due to long lines at the Colosseum, we recommend you begin your tour at the Palatine, where there is never a line to enter and crowds are far less dense. Then continue on to the Forum and Colosseum.

at the base of the Palatine Hill, west of the House of the Vestal Virgins, does fill in some of the blanks of the earliest days of Rome. Also like the hut, it further supports the theory that the city that would become Rome did in fact emerge from humble beginnings on the Palatine Hill and, in fewer than 1,000 years, grow to control the entire Mediterranean, Western Europe, the Isle of Britain, Eastern Europe, the Middle East and the southern half of the Black Sea.

FROM KINGDOM TO REPUBLIC

The Temple of Jupiter Optimus Maximus & the temples of Portunus & Hercules Victor

A timeline of the earliest centuries of Rome is speculative at best, as it relies on sources that, while ancient, were recording a history that had already unfolded hundreds of years in the past. Dionysius of Halicarnassus and Livy, the two major sources for the story of the foundation of Rome, both lived at the turn of the millennium – at least 800 years after Romulus.

While Dionysius' writings dealt primarily with Romulan legend, Livy's *History of Rome,* recorded at the end of the first century BCE, chronicled the history of the city as it evolved from kingdom to republic. The written sources and oral histories Livy relied on would have been created to cast a flattering light on the actions of Rome's most-favoured leaders. Lines were blurred between divine intervention and historical fact, both as a means of reinforcing the concept of Rome's manifest destiny and simply for the sake of telling a better story.

After Romulus' death, Rome is said to have been ruled by a succession of kings, the last three all of Etruscan origin, meaning they came from the region north of Rome that includes present-day northern Lazio (the region of Rome), Umbria and Tuscany (the latter of which takes its name from the Etruscans). Ostensibly to offset the powers of the monarchy, Rome had a Senate, a body which had existed since the time of Romulus. Rome's last king, Etruscan Lucius Tarquinius Superbus, was unpopular with the Roman people and is said to have abused his power and undermined the Senate. He was overthrown and banished from the city and in 509 BCE the Roman Republic was formed. Through civil wars, far-reaching conflicts and conquests of territories throughout Europe, North Africa and the Middle East, the Republic lasted until 27 CE.

While the historicity and chronology

of the Etruscan kings and the formation of the Republic can never be precisely verified, the influence of Etruscan culture on Rome is extensive and demonstrable. From the Etruscans, Rome absorbed its earliest rituals and systems of worship, including its three most important deities: Juno, Minerva and Jupiter, the latter the mythological equivalent of Zeus. From the Etruscans, Romans learned how to build roads and municipal projects (Rome's massive drainage canal, Cloaca Maxima, was built by the Etruscan kings and still empties into the Tiber today) and, most importantly, they learned how to build temples.

The Temple of Jupiter Optimus Maximus

That Livy and Dionysius of Halicarnassus relied on unverifiable sources for their written histories of Rome is certain, but what is also certain is that when these chroniclers were active in Rome, they frequently set eyes on the city's most important ancient temple, around which every significant ritual, political or military event in the history of Rome centred: the Temple of Jupiter Optimus Maximus.

Also known as the Temple of Capitoline Jupiter, the Temple of Jupiter Optimus Maximus – which translates to the Jupiter 'best and greatest' – was a massive structure set at the top of the Capitoline Hill and visible from virtually every part of Rome. It was built on the orders of Lucius Tarquinius Superbus, but would

be dedicated around the time of the formation of the Republic, in 509 BCE. The foundation of the original temple was made of *cappellaccio*, a porous volcanic tufa stone that could be easily quarried and cut. The foundation measured at least 55 x 60 metres, meaning there was simply nothing else in Rome, or in the world known to most Romans, that approached its size.

Though speculation exists as to its design, scholars agree that the temple, raised on a podium, or platform reached via a flight of stairs, followed then contemporary Etruscan design. It had a portico supported by at least four, and more likely six, columns set three or four rows deep. The portico covered the entrances to three cellae, or chambers, each dedicated to a member of the triad: the largest and central cella was for Jupiter, with Juno's to the left and Minerva's to the right.

The earliest temple was likely

Model of the Temple of Juno Optimus Maximus.
Sailko/Wikimedia Commons.

constructed of mud brick covered in stucco, which would have been brightly painted, all the more to make the temple a beacon and symbol for miles around. The roof of the temple was made of terracotta tiles supported by wood beams. The front of the roof had a pediment, or triangular panel, decorated with painted bas-relief (low-relief) sculptures. A terracotta sculpture on the peak of the roof depicted Jupiter driving a chariot drawn by four horses.

Inside the central cella was a cult statue of Jupiter, also in terracotta and painted a deep red. The temple was the symbolic home of the triad of deities, and the statue of Jupiter was a spiritual link to the god himself. When triumphal processions – parades of a victorious general, his legions and the spoils of war, including prisoners destined for slavery or execution – wended their way through the city and along the Via Sacra, their endpoint was the temple. There, the general, his face painted red to match that of the statue, would oversee sacrifices – both human and animal – and leave offerings to Jupiter.

With its status as the most important religious building in Rome, the Temple of Jupiter Optimus Maximus served as a reminder, both to Romans and outsiders, of the pre-eminence of Rome, its ordained-by-the-gods superiority over its rivals, and the permanency and immovability of its dominance.

But the temple itself proved far less immovable. In 83 BCE, during a period

Remains of the podium of the Temple of Juno Optimus Maximus in the Capitoline Museums.
Courtesy Capitoline Museums.

of civil war in Rome, the first temple burned to the ground, leaving only the foundation and podium. A second temple, dedicated in 69 CE, burned down during internecine fighting that same year. The third temple, built by Emperor Vespasian and dedicated in 75 CE, burned down in a widespread fire in 80 CE.

Each reconstruction of the temple was increasingly more elaborate and completed with more expensive materials. The fourth, and final temple – the version that Livy and Dionysius of Halicarnassus would have seen – was the most extravagant, with marble construction, bronze roof tiles, gold-plated doors, marble columns and intricate carvings on the pediment. This iteration of the temple stood until the late fourth century CE, when Emperor Theodosius made Christianity the official religion of Rome and ordered the closing of all pagan places of worship. The Temple of Jupiter fell into a gradual state of disrepair and parts of it were plundered for use in other structures.

Rome was sacked by Vandals in the fifth century, and the temple was further pillaged. It stood in ruins until the 1500s, when it was definitely razed and its materials used to build the Palazzo Caffarelli, which still stands and is now the property of the City of Rome.

Thus Rome's oldest and most important temple has all but vanished. Knowledge of the temple architecture comes from a handful of ancient sources, including coins and relief carvings, and from illustrations predating the palazzo. The majority of the temple foundation lies underneath Palazzo Caffarelli, which is currently closed to the public. In the Palazzo dei Conservatori, one of the twin edifices that make up the Capitoline Museums, sections of the podium and foundation are still visible. Outside the museum, on Via del Tempio di Giove, behind Rome's city government offices, a corner of the temple foundation and podium is preserved under a glass canopy.

HOW TO SEE IT: Located at the top of the Capitoline Hill, the Capitoline Museums (Musei Capitolini) contain sections of the temple and offers didactic information on the structure and its significance to ancient Rome. The museums are open daily from 9.30 am to 7.30 pm. Visit **http://www.museicapitolini.org** for more information.

The Temple of Portunus

Fortunately for modern visitors, not all of Rome's most ancient temples have been reduced to their foundations. The Temple of Portunus was built in the third or fourth century BCE, and its high state of preservation makes it a model for understanding the characteristics of temple design and construction during the Republican era.

Set on land that was once part of the Forum Boarium, the temple was dedicated to Portunus, the god associated with livestock and river travel. The Forum Boarium was the cattle market and mercantile area right at the port of Rome, so the temple served an auspicious purpose in protecting the livestock-laden ships arriving from the Port of Ostia and in ensuring prosperous trade.

The Temple of Portunus was built in the Etruscan style, and can be understood as prototypical of Republican temples, none other of which came close to the scale of the Capitoline Jupiter (discussed above). Although the temple was rebuilt in the first century BCE, its design is thought to follow the original. The temple measures just 10.5 x 19 metres, and sits on a raised podium, from which it would have been visible to arriving ships. It has a *tetrastyle*, or four-column portico and a single *cella*, or interior chamber. The temple sat overlooking a bend in the Tiber, which still flows just yards away but has since been hemmed in with a high stone embankment.

The Temple of Portunus.

The portico is held up by a total of six columns, which are fluted, or incised with channels of equal size. They are topped with ionic capitals, identified by their scroll designs. The remaining twelve columns are 'engaged', or attached to the outer walls of the *cella* and serve no structural purpose. The freestanding columns are made of travertine marble, while the engaged columns and the *cella* are of volcanic tufa, which would have been covered with stucco.

The Tiber River silted up in the first century CE, and the port had to be abandoned. The temple fell into disuse,

Side view of the Temple of Portunus, with engaged columns.

but managed to avoid falling victim to 'spoliage', or the stripping of materials for reuse elsewhere. In the 800s, it was dedicated as a Catholic Christian church, Santa Maria Egyziaca (Saint Mary of Egypt) and its interior was decorated with frescoes depicting the life of the saint. While other ancient monuments in Rome, including the once-mighty Temple of Jupiter Optimus Maximus, the Colosseum and the Circus Maximus, were pillaged for their ornamentation and marble, the Temple of Portunus was spared because it was a Christian place of worship.

The church was deconsecrated in 1921, when it was returned to the State of Italy and efforts began to restore the temple. A

series of major restorations began in 2006 and continued through 2016, and included cleaning and reinforcement of the temple exterior, a roof replacement, and restoration of the early medieval frescoes of the interior. Wherever possible, original building materials were reused.

The Temple of Hercules Victor

One hundred metres from the Temple of Portunus sits the second of Rome's best-preserved Republican temples, that of Hercules Victor. Built around 120 BCE, the temple is thought to have been commissioned to commemorate the Roman military victories in Greece. The temple is of Greek design, and notable for its round shape and that it is the oldest surviving marble building in Rome.

The temple is about 15 metres in diameter, and has a round *cella* ringed by twenty marble columns – nineteen

The Cloaca Maxima as it drains into the Tiber.

The Cloaca Maxima: Rome's ancient sewer

To get a glimpse of one of the world's oldest and longest-functioning sewer systems, walk out on the Ponte Palatino, or Palatine Bridge, reached by crossing Lungotevere Aventino right near the temples of Portunus and Hercules Victor. Once you're on the bridge, look down to your left, back towards the riverbank at the archway set in the embankment wall. This is the drainage canal of the Cloaca Maxima, or 'great sewer', first constructed around 600 BCE. The Cloaca was a central canal built to drain the swamplands of Rome and carry away wastewater. As aqueducts were constructed and Rome's elaborate system of fresh running water developed, they all eventually drained into the Cloaca Maxima. When it was first constructed, the Cloaca was entirely or mostly uncovered; it became a covered, or underground sewer system as structures were built over it. Rainwater and water from Rome's aqueducts flowed through it at a swift pace, as did human and animal waste, garbage and, occasionally, dead bodies. Water still flows out of the Cloaca, albeit at a much slower rate of speed than in ancient times.

The Temple of Hercules Victor.

of them original. The columns are of the Corinthian order, characterised by elaborately carved capitals depicting acanthus leaves and scrolls. The thin fluted columns are nearly 11 metres tall, and their slenderness and close proximity to one another lend a loftiness to the design. The roof of the temple is a later addition and the original design and appearance of the roof is unknown.

As with the Temple of Portunus, conversion to a church in the Middle Ages saved the Temple of Hercules Victor from spoliage. By the 1100s, it had been consecrated as the Church of Santo Stefano alle Carozze (Saint Stephen of the Carriage) and was later rededicated as Santa Maria del Sole, or Saint Mary of the Sun. By the end of the 1800s, the

church had been deconsecrated and efforts began to restore the temple. A complete restoration took place in the 1990s, when the current roof was added.

HOW TO SEE IT: The temples of Portunus and Hercules Victor are located in a grassy patch between two busy roads, Via Luigi Petroselli and Lungotevere Aventino. Both are easily visible, but enclosed by fences and only open by reservation. Individual and group tours are offered on the first and third Sundays of each month, and must be reserved at least twenty-four hours in advance by calling 06/399. 67700.

3

FROM BRICK TO MARBLE

Early Imperial ambitions at the Basilica Julia, Nero's Domus Aurea, and the Colosseum

'Urbem latericium invenit, marmoream reliquit'.
'He found a city of brick; he left a city of marble'.

These words are attributed to Caesar Augustus, the first emperor of Rome, and were etched on his tomb. Though humility may not have been Augustus's strong suit, his self-ascribed epitaph was not inaccurate – in the decades of his rule, Rome undertook ambitious building projects of monumental scale and engineering, with a grandeur befitting the most important city of what was then the most dominant empire of the known world.

The last century BCE would also mark the last century of the Roman Republic. A series of conflicts within Rome and its hinterlands, as well as on its more distant borders, destabilised the Republic in the early decades of the century. As Julius Caesar conquered territories in northern Europe in the name of Rome, he amassed tremendous wealth and influence, and the loyalty of his military legions. His march on Rome in 49 BCE sparked a civil war and further weakened an already faltering republic. Caesar consolidated power and engineered to have himself declared

dictator for life, effectively ending the republican form of government.

Julius Caesar's assassination on the Ides of March, 44 BCE, was an effort by a group of conspiring senators to restore the Republic. Instead, it prolonged the civil wars for several years. In his will, Caesar adopted his grand-nephew, Octavian, as his son and sole heir, thus legitimising the latter's claim as successor of Caesar. Years of war and conflict culminated in 31 BCE, when Octavian defeated Mark Antony and Cleopatra at Actium, Greece. Though it would be a few years before Octavian was declared by the Senate 'Augustus', or 'illustrious one' – he later also adopted the title Imperator Caesar – 31 BCE is considered the definitive end of the Republic and the beginning of the reign of Caesar Augustus, the first emperor of the Roman Empire.

Basilica Julia

When Julius Caesar died, he left behind several unfinished building projects, which Augustus completed on an even grander scale. One of the most important of these was the Basilica Julia, a large public building on the Roman Forum, the low-lying area between the Palatine and Capitoline hills that for more than 1,000 years was the centre of Roman commercial, political and social life.

Although 'basilica' is a term most commonly associated with Christian Catholic churches, its concept and design originated with the Romans. A basilica was a large, rectangular building with a central nave, or hall, flanked by two or four aisles. The space was intended to accommodate large groups of people and for this reason, its design was later appropriated by the church. But the original basilica model was that of a public, or municipal building, typically the site of civil court hearings, government and banking offices, and, frequently, small shops. Unlike its later manifestations, the Roman basilica had no religious function and was very much the centre of public life in the city. For perspective, there are the ruins of seven basilicas on the Roman Forum alone, several of which were contemporaneously in use.

Julius Caesar began construction of a basilica to replace a Republican-era

Model of the Basilica Julia.
Lasha Tskhondia/
L_VII_C_Creative Commons

Ancient graffiti

Etched into the steps of the Basilica Julia, archaeologists have found traces of ancient games, including a grid similar to a checker- or chessboard—presumably left behind by bored Romans passing time as they waited on official business.

one at the same location, near the base of the Capitoline Hill. When Augustus finished the basilica after Caesar's death, he dedicated it to his adopted father, hence the Basilica Julia. More than just a posthumous honour, naming the basilica after Caesar was a symbolic political gesture intended to remind Romans of Augustus' connection to his revered uncle/father, whom by 42 BCE had been deified. Augustus' many titles included 'son of the Divine One' – and therefore divine himself.

The basilica measured 101 x 49 metres and was three storeys tall at its centre. Its central hall, or nave, was 82 x 18 metres, and was surrounded on all four sides by three rows of pillars with engaged columns, which supported the roof and also created two aisles all around the nave. While the nave was open to the ceiling, the aisles were two-storey, with the top floor likely reserved for offices or for spectators to observe the proceedings below. Contemporary writers recalled that four court cases could be heard simultaneously in the basilica—we must imagine that all day long, it would have been somewhat

chaotic, crowded with people moving about, and buzzing with commercial and municipal activity.

The basilica sat on a low, raised podium, with steps on at least three sides. Its exterior was composed of rows of arches supported by pillars. It was the perfection of the arch that made possible buildings on the scale of the Basilica Julia and permitted the lofty open space central to its design. While the true arch, that is, a rounded arch with a keystone at its centre, was an architectural innovation inherited from the Etruscans, the Romans exploited it like no other culture before them, using it to distribute the weight and create vaulted spaces as their buildings rose ever-higher.

Shortly after its completion, the Basilica Julia was destroyed by a fire in either 12 or 9 BCE, then rebuilt and rededicated in 2 BCE. The basilica underwent renovations and repairs over the centuries, but survived more-or-less intact until 410 CE, when the Visigoths sacked Rome. Though repairs were made in 416, Rome was by then a city on the decline; the basilica fell into disuse, other than serving as a church during the early Middle Ages. Eventually it, like so many of Rome's grand imperial structures, was used as a quarry for marble, brick and travertine.

Today the Basilica Julia is part of the picturesque landscape of ruins that comprise the Roman Forum. The stepped podium remains, if only in outline,

Ruins of the Basilica Julia show the footprint of the structure, with central nave and aisles delineated by brick pillar bases.

allowing modern-day visitors to visualise the footprint of the basilica. In what would have been the nave, bits of the marble pavement, which once dazzled with colour and intricacy, peek out from the grass. Column and pillar bases are still in place, so the pattern of the nave and aisles is clear. A portion of a single marble column still stands, re-erected in the nineteenth century. All around the ruin, fragments of columns and capitals lay haphazardly.

At what would have been the south-west corner of the basilica, in the section closest to the Capitoline, a corner wall with arches, as well as a portion of the aisle, is visible. In the aisle, at the top of the brick pillars begin the curve of the arches that would have formed the ceiling structure – consider this is just the first floor. On the far western side, wedges of brick at the top of each pillar once held marble statues.

The original basilica was constructed of *opus caementicium*, or Roman cement (see sidebar, p38), which was clad in brick, travertine or marble. A third-century CE reconstruction by Emperor

The remains of an aisle on the south-west side of the Basilica Julia.

Diocletian—again as the result of a devastating fire, this time in 283—meant that walls were rebuilt entirely in brick. While the dimensions and design of the third-century phase are thought to have been in keeping with the original scheme, the Augustan basilica was very likely a much more opulent space than its later iterations.

The south-west corner of the basilica survived, relatively speaking, because the church built into that small section of the building in the seventh or eighth century CE was not subject to spoliage. Despite its poor state of preservation today, the significance and scale of this monumental building demonstrate well the ambitions of Augustus' building initiatives—to dazzle Romans and visitors alike with a massive display of the engineering capabilities of the new empire, to overwhelm with dimensions never before seen, and to impress with

HOW TO SEE IT: To the remains of the Basilica Julia are within the Roman Forum archaeological area. A combined ticket includes admission to the Palatine, the Colosseum and the Roman Forum. The site opens at 8:30 am and remains open until 4:30 or 5 pm during winter months, and until 7:15 pm during peak summer season. Check **https://www.coopculture.it/en/heritage.cfm?id=4** for current information.

the extreme wealth that was required to realize such a project.

The Domus Aurea

Augustus and his successors brought to the Roman public architecture on a scale and splendour that had never before been seen. Yet privately, Augustus and his wife Livia were said to have lived in relatively modest surroundings – for an emperor, at least. The *Domus Augusti*, or House of Augustus, sat on the western edge of the Palatine Hill, its position strategically selected for its proximity to the Casa Romuli and sacred sites associated with the founding of Rome. There, in two side-by-side houses, Augustus and Livia had large public receiving-rooms decorated in an austere manner. Separate from these was a section of private chambers, including bedrooms, studies and guest quarters, which were small and brilliantly adorned with colourful wall paintings, many of which have been brought back to life through ongoing restorations. While Augustus and his wife presumably lived with every comfort and luxury, he saved the grandeur and ostentation for religious and municipal buildings that everyday Romans would see, and that would remind them of his benevolent and paternalistic role as the father of Rome.

Augustus' great-great grandson, Nero (his full title was Nero Claudius Caesar Augustus Germanicus) was the fifth emperor of Rome (54-68 CE), and the last member of the Julio-Claudian dynasty to rule the empire. Nero's name evokes images of a crazed despot, though recent reconsiderations suggests a more complicated legacy – of a charismatic, complex and quite possibly mentally ill leader who was popular with the common people, reviled by the Senate and upper classes, and historicised as a tyrant in accounts written in the years after his death. Stories of his cruelty and depravity, from fiddling while Rome burned to sacrificing Christians to lions to murdering his mother, stepbrother and at least one of his wives, range from probably true (the murders) to patently false (the fiddling).

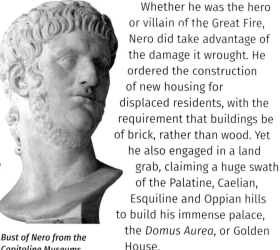

Bust of Nero from the Capitoline Museums.
Image: CC BY-SA 3.0/Creative Commons

The Great Fire of AD 64 started on the Aventine Hill, where narrow, winding streets of densely-built wooden houses quickly went up in flames. It burned for more than a week, and swept across the Forum, Capitoline and Palatine Hills. Palaces, temples and wealthy residences were destroyed as readily as the slum-like districts of the Suburra, the area north-east of the Forum. Nero is claimed by various accounts to have: ordered the starting of the fire, prevented fire brigades from extinguishing it, opened up his garden and palaces to the homeless, and helped search for survivors in the aftermath.

Whether he was the hero or villain of the Great Fire, Nero did take advantage of the damage it wrought. He ordered the construction of new housing for displaced residents, with the requirement that buildings be of brick, rather than wood. Yet he also engaged in a land grab, claiming a huge swath of the Palatine, Caelian, Esquiline and Oppian hills to build his immense palace, the *Domus Aurea*, or Golden House.

The Domus Aurea covered an estimated area of more than 300 acres, with a complex that included 300 rooms, and acres of gardens, pastures and vineyards. On the shores of an artificial lake – where the Colosseum would be later built – were stage-set type facades of the great cities of the empire. The exterior of the palace, decorated in gold leaf (aurea means gold), was said to have glimmered in the sun.

The interior of the palace was clad in every precious material available, with marble floors and walls, and mosaics on floors and ceilings. Jewels, ivory, pearls and mother-of-pearl were embedded into some walls and ceilings, while most were richly decorated with colourful frescoes. Rooms were filled with fountains, shallow pools, ornate furnishings and statuary.

Fresco fragments in a vaulted ceiling of the Domus Aurea. Sébastien Amiet/CC BY-SA 2.0/Creative Commons

Architecturally, the Domus Aurea was significant not just for its size, but for its innovation. Up until this point, concrete had been used as a structural element, to bulk up loadbearing walls and form the core of pillars. At the Domus Aurea it was used for aesthetic purposes, to build barrel vaults and domed ceilings, and to create niches for statues. The domus's octagonal court had a domed ceiling with a large oculus at its centre – an innovation that would be perfected a century later at the Pantheon. To the astonishment of guests and nearly two millennia later, archaeologists, the Domus Aurea's grand dining hall was built on a rotating platform. It turned constantly as guests gazed up at a changing motif of day to night on its domed ceiling. At intervals during a dinner, ivory panels in the ceiling would slide open to shower perfume and rose petals on guests below.

Upon completion of the Domus Aurea in 68 CE, Nero is said to have exclaimed, 'I can at last begin to live like a human being!'

But his enjoyment of the pleasure palace would be short-lived. Nero nearly bankrupted Rome to build the Domus, and the ostentation of the palace was

A Domus Aurea guide points to a spoliage hole in the ceiling of a frescoed room.

too much, even for a Senate accustomed to imperial excesses. His extravagances at the Domus Aurea, combined with his hedonistic lifestyle and flaunting of imperial protocols, turned the Senate and the wealthy class of Rome against him. In the days before his death, Nero had fled several miles from Rome. Upon hearing that the Senate had declared him a public enemy and that he would face execution when he returned to Rome, he killed himself in June of 68, the same year the Domus Aurea was completed.

After his death, the Senate declared *damnatio memoriae*, or 'condemnation of memory' of Nero. That meant his memory and legacy were to be erased, though in practice, it was only a partial scrubbing of the record. While coins of Nero remained in circulation and several portrait busts survived, the Domus Aurea did not. The palace was stripped of its gold, jewels and artwork, and its soaring, vaulted rooms were completely filled-in with millions of tonnes of rubble. Remaining parts of the palace were incorporated into other structures. In the space of just over ten years, its lake would transform into

the Colosseum and eventually, the Domus Aurea was forgotten.

The Domus Aurea remained buried until the Renaissance era, when it became a curiosity for artists like Michelangelo and Raphael, who would lower themselves on ropes into the buried 'grottoes' of the domus to observe the fantastical frescoes – the term 'grotesque' – *grotto-esque* – comes from here. Haphazard excavations took place over the centuries, but it wasn't until the late twentieth century that systematic study and preservation of the ruins was undertaken.

Fortunately for modern visitors, the *damnatio memoriae* of Nero meant that large sections of the Domus Aurea could be excavated and open to the public. Although it includes just a small section of the vast complex, a tour of the open rooms provides a sense of the grandeur of the palace, particularly the height of its ceilings and loftiness of its chambers, which were once flooded with natural light. It provides one of the most complete pictures of the scale and technological prowess of Imperial architecture, and offers fascinating insight into Rome's most complex and infamous emperor.

HOW TO SEE IT: The entrance to the Domus Aurea is in the Parco delle Colle Oppio, in the area immediately north-north-east of the Colosseum. Guided tours of the Domus Aurea include a virtual reality experience that vividly recreates the palace as it looked in Nero's time. Tours are currently offered Saturdays and Sundays only, and may sell out weeks in advance. Visit **www.coopculture.it/en** for more information and to book a tour.

The Colosseum

Following the death and *damnatio memoriae* of Nero, his eventual successor, Vespasian, undertook projects intended to return lands seized by Nero for the Domus Aurea to the people of Rome. Foremost among these was the Flavian Amphitheatre, better known as the Colosseum, which was named for the Flavian dynasty, which included emperors Vespasian, Titus and Domitian. Vespasian's choice to set the amphitheatre in the centre of Rome was a political move meant to symbolize the largest of the new imperial dynasty and further eradicate Nero's legacy.

The project to build the world's largest arena was funded from the spoils of the First Roman-Jewish War, which ended with the complete destruction of much of the city of Jerusalem and the burning and pillaging of its Second Temple, Judea's most important religious complex. More than 100,000 Jews were brought to Rome as slaves, and tens of thousands of them were used as forced labour to build the Colosseum.

The gruesome nature of the Colosseum is well known and undisputed. Hundreds of thousands of people and millions of wild animals – sometimes thousands in a single day – were killed there in bloody spectacles, brutal executions, gladiatorial fights and staged hunts.

It's difficult today to understand the bloodlust that drove Roman spectators by the tens of thousands to the Colosseum. Why would they delight in the sadistic slaughter of terrified animals, criminals or prisoners of war, or cheer for the death of a stricken gladiator? The Colosseum has to be considered as representative of the Roman Empire at its most powerful: it had subjugated most of the known world, subjected those who resisted, tamed wild beasts and conquered

Nero's Colossal Ego

The Colosseum earned its name from a 30-metre bronze statue of Nero which once stood at the entrance to the Domus Aurea. After Nero's death the head of the statue was refashioned as the sun god, Sol, and it was moved to a site adjacent to the Flavian Amphitheatre, where it remained for several centuries afterward. The statue was known as the *Colosso*, and the nickname for the amphitheatre stuck.

The Colosseum.

exotic, far-flung lands. The hunts, the ritual executions and the gladiatorial combats were the physical, depravedly gory embodiment of that dominance. But if you were watching the bloodshed, even if you were a plebeian or a slave on the lowest rungs of Roman society, you were on the winning side.

Today, the Colosseum is the most popular attraction in Italy – in 2017 it received more than 7 million visitors. It's an internationally recognised icon that is a symbol of Rome itself. While the gory legacy of the Colosseum undoubtedly contributes to its appeal for modern tourists – and those

centuries before them – it is also an architectural achievement unparalleled in the world.

For an initial understanding of the design of the Colosseum, consider it as two semi-circular Roman theatres set facing one another (see Sidebar p.35) to form an oval shaped arena. While the freestanding arena model was not new to Roman architects, the Colosseum was their largest, tallest undertaking to date, and remains the largest arena of the ancient world. It originally measured 545 metres in circumference and nearly 50 metres tall. Its three main levels were composed of eighty arches, which were supported by pillars and half-columns. The arches on the second and third floors held statues, most likely of mythological figures, deities and past emperors. The fourth level, called an attic, was a later addition ordered by Emperor Diocletian. Instead of arches this level had windows, as well as a row of 240 sockets, which held wood masts over which a protective awning could be unfurled on particularly sunny days.

The Colosseum had interior and exterior ring walls supported by vaulted porticos. The corridors created by these two walls allowed access to stairs and different, numbered exits and seating areas. The seating levels were divided by social hierarchy – with the ancient equivalent of premium box seats for emperors and Vestal Virgins. Members of the senate sat outside the boxes but at the same level. Heading up from there were seats for the Roman public. Lower seats and better views were reserved for wealthier Romans – the higher up spectators were, the lower their economic or social standing. Slaves, women and poor people were relegated to wooden benches on the fourth level, which was the highest and least comfortable.

Like modern arenas, entry and exit doors and stairs were numbered, and each spectator was given the ancient equivalent of a ticket – a numbered tesserae, or terracotta tile, that directed them to the correct doorway, stairs and level. It is said that the arena, which

The Theatre of Marcellus.

Colosseum Prototype

If you walk from the Capitoline Hill towards the Jewish Ghetto and the Portico of Ottavia, you'll see a building whose exterior looks a lot like the Colosseum. And that's no coincidence. The Teatro di Marcello, or Theatre of Marcellus, was built on a semi-circular plan, as were all Roman theatres. Roman theatres were already a departure from the Greek models which were built into hillsides or on sloping landscapes. Use of cement, arches and vaulted arcades allowed Roman architects to create free-standing theatres that were supported by their own bulky foundations. Initiated by Julius Caesar and completed by Augustus in 13 BCE, the Theatre of Marcellus was the largest of its time. The Colosseum follows its model of a level of Doric columns, then a level of Ionic columns and what was presumably a top level of Corinthian columns—though these are no longer present at the theatre. Today only a portion of the façade is visible to passers-by, and the interior and upper floors of the theatre are some of Rome's most exclusive private residences. But the extant façade makes clear from where the Colosseums' architects took their inspiration.

The remains of the Colosseum underground, the network of passageways and cells under the oval floor. Above are remains of the arena's tiered seating.

held an estimated 50,000 spectators, could be emptied of crowds within 10 minutes.

The oval floor of the arena measured 87 x 5 metres and was ringed by a 5-metre-tall wall. The floor was made of wood planks, and covered with sand – which absorbed blood and could be easily cleaned between spectacles. Underneath the floor was the hypogeum, a complicated, two-level labyrinth of chambers, hallways, stairs and ramps, which allowed scenery, wild animals and criminals about to be executed to enter the arena from underground. There were two gates, or doors, to access the arena at ground level. Gladiators entered through one – the other was reserved for transporting their dead bodies off the floor.

The Colosseum was used for gladiatorial games and executions – the latter often elaborately protracted – into the sixth century. A fire and an earthquake, in the third and fifth centuries, respectively, required extensive rebuilding of the arena. In tandem with the fortunes of the empire, as Rome fell so fell the Colosseum. After the last games were held in 523,

the arena fell into disuse and neglect. The interior was used as a stone quarry, and the exterior, which was once clad in more than 100,000 cubic metres of travertine, held in place with iron clamps, was stripped away – pockmarks in the remaining façade show where the iron was pried away for reuse elsewhere. A series of earthquakes did further damage, except there was no

Cementing the Empire: The development of Roman concrete

The architectural and engineering feats achieved during the late Republican and early Imperial Roman periods can be attributed to one construction material, *opus caementicium*, or Roman concrete, which first appeared on the scene at the beginning of the second century BCE. While cement itself was not a new material for erecting walls of tufa or travertine, Romans unleashed an innovation by using volcanic sand, called *pozzolana*, which they mined in the area surrounding Mount Vesuvius, near the modern city of Naples. The *pozzolana* (instead of regular sand) was mixed with lime and when water was added it created a strong, cohesive mortar that actually grew stronger over time.

Initially, *opus caementicium* was used primarily as mortar and fill for walls, then increasingly, as buildings became larger and more elaborate, as the core of pillars. As Roman engineers realized the strength and versatility of the material, they began to exploit its possibilities and create buildings that were much grander, taller and more ambitious. The Domus Aurea shows us how *opus caementicium* first began being used aesthetically, while the enduring arches of the Colosseum and the elegant oculus of the Pantheon (see Chapter 4) remind us of the incredible durability of the cement that revolutionized Roman architecture.

Oculus on the top of Pantheon.

longer a wealthy empire to bankroll repairs.

The centuries of the Middle Ages saw the crumbling Colosseum used as a vegetable garden and a cow pasture, as workshops, and as a twelfth-century fortress. An earthquake in 1349 caused most of the exterior wall on the south side to collapse and the rubble was used as building material elsewhere in the city. The travertine facing was stripped, and most often burned to make lime for mixing cement. Today, only a portion of the exterior ring is still standing – on many of the thirty-one remaining arches, the Roman numerals that directed tesserae holders to the seats are still visible.

From the mid-1700s, the arena was deemed a sacred site, beginning the Colosseum's association with Christian

sacrifices, despite no conclusive evidence that anyone was ever executed there specifically because of their religion. From this point onward, the Colosseum was no longer used for spoliage. Serious restoration efforts began in the nineteenth century, as evidenced by the brick wedges that hold up either end of the perimeter wall fragment. Restorations and excavations continue today, with each successive project yielding a greater understanding of the ancient world's most spectacular arena.

HOW TO SEE IT: A combined ticket includes admission to the Colosseum, the Roman Forum and the Palatine Hill. The site opens at 8:30 am and remains open until 4:30 or 5 pm during winter months, and until 7:15 pm during peak summer season. Check **https://www.coopculture.it/en** for current information.

Entrance to the Colosseum is via timed entry. While a limited number of same-day tickets are available, we strongly recommend that you purchase tickets in advance via the Coopculture website (**https://www.coopculture.it/en/**). Weeks or months in advance is not too soon to purchase, especially during peak season. You may also wish to consider one of dozens of options for a guided tour.

THE APEX OF EMPIRE
Trajan's Markets, the Pantheon, and the Baths of Caracalla

By the time the fourth tier of the Colosseum was set in place in the late first century CE, Rome was in the midst of a full-blown architectural revolution. The Classical order and symmetry appropriated from the Greeks had melded with the engineering and aesthetic possibilities of arches, vaults and cement, and Roman architects exploited these potentials to the utmost.

Rome's military dominance across Europe, the Mediterranean, North Africa and the Near East meant that public and private architecture was well-funded, the hands to build it – in the form of slave labour – were plentiful, and innovation and experimentation were encouraged by emperors and wealthy patrons intent on leaving an enduring mark on the city's landscape.

The opening of the second century CE began what is considered the Empire's peak period of prosperity and supremacy. It's marked by the period of the 'Five Good Emperors,' so-called because of the stability and egalitarianism – the latter at least for Roman citizens and allies – with which they reigned. Though the borders of the Empire were aggressively expanded and defended during this century, in Rome, at least, daily life was predictable

and reasonably safe, even if the quality of one's life was strictly determined by social caste. It was also during this period of time that some of Rome's most monumental, ambitious and enduring public building projects were undertaken. At a time when the vast majority of Rome's more than one million residents lived in dark, cramped quarters, the grand public spaces created during this era provided not only (and quite literally) breathing room, but a reminder – just as the games of the Colosseum were a reminder – of the powerful empire of which they were privileged to be a part.

Trajan's Market

Second in the succession of 'Good Emperors' (following Nerva, who ruled for just two years before his death), Trajan was emperor from 98 to 117 CE.

Trajan's Column, with the remains of the Basilica Ulpia below.

Distinguished for his successful military campaigns in Dacia (modern Romania), Trajan was already popular with the Roman people when he became emperor. His massive building project, the Forum of Trajan, commemorated his military triumphs, particularly in Dacia, and contained the grand Basilica Ulpia, two libraries, and a richly decorated portico. The 30-metre tall, marble victory column that depicts the Dacian campaign in carved relief is still a landmark in the centre of Rome.

Standing at the foot of Trajan's Column and looking south-west, the partially restored columns of the Basilica Ulpia are beneath the column, ringed by the remains of the portico that surrounded the basilica. To the immediate right, the Via dei Fori Imperiali, a four-lane road inaugurated in 1932 by Mussolini, covers a wide swath of Trajan's Forum. And to the left, a hemicycle (semi-circular), three-storey brick building forms the remains of the Markets of Trajan, colloquially known as the 'world's first shopping mall'.

Rome's conquest of Egypt and the Middle East meant that it controlled the eastern portions of the Silk Road, the vast ancient trade network that transported merchandise between India, Asia, Africa, and Europe. Roman artefacts, most notably glassware, have been found at archaeological sites as far away as India, Korea, China

The hemicycle-shaped Markets of Trajan, seen from Via dei Fori Imperiali.

Via Biberatica, or the 'Drinking Street' at the Markets of Trajan. Carole Raddato/CC2.0/Flickr

and Vietnam. Romans, in turn, coveted the silk and spices from these exotic and unimaginably long-distance trading partners. The marketplace, commissioned by Trajan and designed by his preferred architect, Apollodorus of Damascus, was a symbolic microcosm of second-century Rome – the greatest commercial complex of the greatest of all empires (and the greatest of all emperors) – contained under one roof.

Constructed from about 100–110 CE, the three-level complex was 35 metres tall and was set into the side of the Quirinal Hill. At the ground level, it opened onto the Forum of Trajan, while a road, Via Biberatica (which roughly means 'the drinking street' – so named for the number of taverns along this span) ran along the back of the upper level. The market's semi-circular shape was adapted to follow the contour of the forum, which predates it. The brick buildings on top of the hemicycle are medieval additions – the original shop, or *taberna*, halls were on the two lower, extant levels. This section consisted of hundreds of small, one-room *tabernae*, which opened onto a covered arcade. Each shop had a wooden door with could be locked at night – still evident by the grooves on the floor where the doors would have slid open and shut. Interior staircases on each end of the hemicycle connected the levels.

Across the Via Biberatica, an open-air market hall was covered by a vaulted roof. Its central hall was open to the ceiling and was flanked by two storeys of rooms used as shops, offices or for other commercial purposes. The entire structure – both the market hall and the arcaded hemicycle, were constructed of cement faced with brick, travertine and stucco. Decorative brickwork, set in herringbone patterns, false arches and alternating forms of brick offered visual variety and loftiness, while white stucco added light.

We have to imagine the Markets of Trajan as a noisy honeycomb of activity, abuzz with buyers and sellers of every imaginable trade good available and the aromas, colours, costume and languages

of the farthest reaches of the world. For the wealthiest Romans, it was the source of all the finery with which they adorned themselves and their elegant homes, proof that money really could buy everything in the world. For the poorest Romans, accustomed to the narrow, fetid streets of Suburra and other slum-like districts, the markets must have seemed like the Roman Empire itself – enormous, wonder-filled, and full of exoticism, temptation and aspiration, and, also like Rome, in the business of making money.

Today, the Markets and Forum of Trajan form the Mercati di Traiano/ Museo dei Fori Imperiali, a museum complex that connects the markets and part of the Imperial Forums, and

The market hall, now exhibition space for the Mercati di Traiano/Museo dei Fori Imperiali.
Carole Raddato/CC2.0/Wikimedia Commons

The Mercati di Traiano/Museo dei Fori Imperiali.
Szilas/CC2.0/Wikimedia Commons

HOW TO SEE IT: You can look out over Trajan's Forum and the Markets of Trajan and get a close-up look at the reliefs of Trajan's Column from Via dei Fori Imperiali, at the stretch of road near Piazza Venezia. To go inside the museum and market buildings – an experience I highly recommend – visit **http://www.mercatiditraiano.it/en**. The museum is open daily from 9.30 am – 7.30 pm, with last entry one hour before closing.

provides helpful context to the daily functions of the commercial, civic and religious precincts affiliated with the sites. Compared to many of Rome's better known attractions, here, visitors can wander the ruins in relative solitude as they peek into ancient shops, climb the same stairs that Roman merchants and consumers climbed nearly 2,000 years ago, and imagine the sights, smells and sounds of the ancient world's busiest international shopping mall.

HOW THE OTHER HALF LIVED, ROMAN-STYLE

Thousands of tourists a day walk right past one of Rome's most fascinating and best-interpreted archaeological sites, Le Domus Romane di Palazzo Valentini. Located in the basement of a sixteenth-century palace and entered near the base of Trajan's Column, Le Domus Romane are a group of houses, which, based on the richness of their remains, belonged to very wealthy residents of Imperial Rome. A riveting multimedia experience brings to colourful life the mosaics, frescoes, polychrome floors, pools and fountains of these

Palazzo Valentini. LPLT/CC3.0/Wikimedia Commons

noble structures, and places them, as well as the surrounding Trajan-era structures, in their historic and geographic context. Entrance is by guided tour only, and it's best to book ahead for this not-to-be-missed look at the lifestyles and environs of Rome's wealthiest echelon. Visit **https://www.palazzovalentini.it/domus-romane/index-en.html** for information.

The Pantheon

M·AGRIPPA·L·F·COS·TERTIVM·FECIT.
The inscription on the front of the Pantheon is immodest, and also a little misleading. It essentially translates to 'Marcus Agrippa built this'. Agrippa was a statesman, consul, general, and, most importantly, son-in-law and closest confidant of Augustus. As a general, he won decisive victories with Augustus' legions and as a politician and strategist, he helped consolidate Augustus' power and install him as the first Emperor of Rome. Agrippa was also an architect, and he designed and oversaw the construction of the earliest iteration of the Pantheon in the first century BCE, built to honour Augustus' victory over Antony and Cleopatra at the Battle of Actium.

Scant evidence remains of the first temple. It was destroyed by fire around 80 CE, and rebuilt by Emperor Domitian. Fire struck again in 110 CE and this time, Trajan undertook reconstruction. Stamped bricks at the site date to Trajan's era, so work was already well underway, though unfinished, when he died in 117 CE. Trajan's successor, Hadrian, oversaw its completion. Third of the 'Five Good Emperors', Hadrian was a patron of the arts and architecture, and an architect himself. He commissioned religious, domestic and municipal building projects – including a rather famous wall spanning the width of Britain – across what was now a vast empire. On the architectural landscape of the city of Rome, the Pantheon is doubtlessly his greatest and most enduring contribution. That he included the inscription which credited its original architect, Agrippa, was intended to symbolise his modesty and piety – both traits not typically associated with Roman emperors.

The Agrippa inscription on the Pantheon.

While it was once thought that the Pantheon of Hadrian, completed between 118 and 128 CE, bore little to no resemblance to the Pantheon of Agrippa, recent research has called into question that thinking. Early scholars surmised that Agrippa's temple was a simple, small rectangular plan, when in fact it might have been a more complex design with dimensions and features closer to those of the Hadrianic structure, including a portico and a circular hall, or rotunda. So perhaps in attributing the building to Agrippa, Hadrian was demonstrating not just piety (whether genuine or feigned) but honesty as well.

What is certain about the second-century Pantheon is that it was revolutionary in its design and construction. While its portico supported by free-standing columns was not new to Roman monumental structures (starting with the Temple of Jupiter Optimus Maximus, Chapter

The portico of the Pantheon. Sailko/CC3.0/Wikimedia Commons

2), these Corinthian columns were more than 12 metres high and were made of monolithic Egyptian granite – unlike typical columns formed of sections of poured concrete cylinders fused together and clad in brick and travertine, these were solid stone. Built in the wake of Augustus and Agrippa's defeat of Antony and Cleopatra, it's no coincidence that the Pantheon incorporated these massive components quarried in Egypt – now another of Rome's vassals.

The interior of the Pantheon was – and is – tremendously innovative and daring. Consider the geometrical perfection of a perfect sphere resting on a cylinder, which supports the world's largest and oldest unreinforced concrete dome. The height of the dome, 43 metres, is equal to its diameter and were it an actual sphere, its bottom would just graze the floor. The structure is composed of concrete faced with brick, with coffers formed in the rotunda to lighten its mass. While the interior of the dome forms a perfect half-circle, if we could see the roof from a bird's-eye-view, we'd see not a semi-circular but a more oval shape – the roof is formed of stepped rings of concrete, each smaller and thinner than the other, leading up

The stepped dome of the Pantheon. Anthony Majanlahti/CC2.0

The oculus of the Pantheon.

to the top of the dome with its famous oculus.

At nearly 8 metres wide, its majestic circular oculus, or skylight, is the building's only source of natural light. Though obviously practical in this sense, the oculus had a symbolic purpose as well – as a window to the heavens, it joined the mortal to the divine, and sitting emperors to deified emperors to the gods themselves. Because the Pantheon was built on the spot where Romulus was allegedly lifted up into the afterlife, the oculus symbolised the window through which he was transported, the continuity of the foundation myth and the seamless connection between the sitting emperor and the first father of Rome.

While the word Pantheon essentially means 'temple of all gods', archaeologists believe that the Agrippa-era structure, built to commemorate

Take a moment to be dazzled

Second to the Colosseum, the Pantheon is the most recognised building in Rome. And winding through the maze of centro storico streets and emerging onto Piazza della Rotunda, the square where the Pantheon sits, and gazing at the front of this exquisitely preserved, 2,000-year-old temple remains one of the most breath-taking experiences in travel. I've stumbled across it hundreds of times, and it still bowls me over.

the victory at Actium, was also intended as a sanctuary to Julius Caesar, a sacred space that further linked him to Augustus and Augustus to the gods themselves. The concept of emperor as god was taking hold – remember that Augustus gave himself the title 'Son of the Divine One' – and the Pantheon provided a setting in which Caesar could be worshipped at a level of importance with the gods themselves. During the early decades of the Pantheon,

the niches at the top of the drum, or cylindrical section of the rotunda, held statues of the gods. By Hadrian's era, when the deification of emperors was part and parcel of Roman political and religious life, the statues of the gods were replaced with statues of past emperors.

As Rome began to decline in the 400s, so did the significance of the Pantheon. In 613 CE, the Byzantine Emperor Phocas granted the Pantheon to Pope Boniface IV, for the purpose of converting it from a pagan site to a church, which would eventually be known as Santa Maria della Rotunda. It is because of this seventh-century conversion that the Pantheon remains in such an excellent state of preservation, though its original gold and bronze cladding and marble statuary were lost to spoliage along the way. Still, on its exterior and interior, the Pantheon today is a building that Hadrian would know, even if the precinct around it would be completely unrecognisable to him.

Present-day visitors to the Pantheon still pass between those massive

Egyptian granite columns and under the portico inscribed with Agrippa's name. They enter through fifteenth-century bronze doors not dissimilar to the original. They walk on the same marble floors, with their colourful circle and square pattern, and see the same walls and niches covered in marble. And they gaze up at the same coffered ceiling and at the light of the same oculus – unchanged since the second century.

The Baths of Caracalla

The death of Marcus Aurelius in 180 CE marked the end of the era of the Five Good Emperors, and also the climax of Rome's most peaceful, prosperous period. Though the borders of the Empire expanded during the 193–211 reign of Septimus Severus, his campaigns drained Rome's coffers, and his attempts to have his two sons, Caracalla and Geta, serve as co-emperors had calamitous results that further destabilised the state.

In 211, Caracalla had Geta murdered – in the presence of their mother – and had thousands of his enemies and political rivals executed. He ordered the damnatio memoriae of Geta, whose image was struck from coins, monuments and the triumphal arch of Septimius Severus, which still stands in the Roman Forum. Caracalla lived in constant fear of assassination and spent the remainder of his reign on military campaigns far from Rome. To ensure the loyalty of the legions, he raised soldiers'

HOW TO SEE IT: The Pantheon is set in the heart of Rome's centro storico, and is open daily from Monday to Saturday from 8.30 am to 7.30 pm (Sundays 9 am to 6 pm). Admission is currently fre. For more information, visit http://www.pantheon-rome.com.

Remains of the Baths of Caracalla, with supporting pillars of the domed calidarium. Image: PCDazero/CC0

Bust of Caracalla. Museo Archeologico Nazionale di Napoli/CC2.5

salaries, but sunk the Empire further into debt in the process. He made citizens of all freed men in all Roman territories, ostensibly an egalitarian move, but more likely so that these new citizens would pay taxes and relieve Rome's debt. His lasting mark on the Roman landscape was another attempt to endear himself to the public, and was one of the last great building projects of the Roman Empire – the Baths of Caracalla.

Though the bath complex was likely initiated by Severus, primary construction took place under Caracalla.

The site for the sprawling bath complex, then the city's largest, was in the southern part of Rome, where there was enough undeveloped space for such a large project (which would ultimately cover about twenty-five hectares). The position at the end of the Appian Way meant that visitors, immediately upon entering Rome, would be astounded by the scale of the complex and the vision and capability of the Empire and, more practically, could also clean themselves before going on to the city. Most importantly, the new baths were in proximity to the Aqua Marcia aqueduct, which would provide a steady supply of clean, free-flowing water for thousands of bathers every day.

At least 21 million bricks and 6,300 cubic metres of marble were used to construct the baths, which were built by a combination of slave and skilled labourers. The central bath building was 44 metres tall and measured 214 by 114 metres. Inaugurated in 216 as the Thermae Antonianae, but familiarly known as the Baths of Caracalla, the main complex consisted of an Olympic-size swimming pool, which was uncovered, plus a wide corridor connecting to cold, tepid, warm and hot baths, plus steam rooms. Side rooms and adjacent buildings contained changing areas and lockers, a

Mosaic floors at the Baths of Caracalla. Pascal Reusch/CC3.0

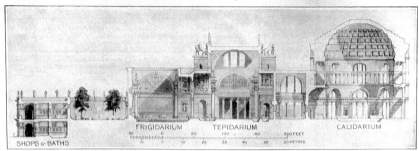

FRIGIDARIUM TEPIDARIUM CALIDARIUM

SHOPS & BATHS

The Magnificent Baths of Caracalla at Rome shown in section (restored) This and the other pictures will appear in the new edition of Sir Banister Fletcher's book

THE MARVELLOUS BATHS of the ROMANS
DESCRIBED BY SIR BANISTER FLETCHER, F.R.I.B.A.

1924 illustration of the Baths of Caracalla. Wellcome Images/CC4.0

gymnasium with weightlifting facilities, and areas for massages and relaxation. In another section of the complex, a market-like area offered taverns, shops, salons and libraries, while outdoors, there were sports fields, a running track, gardens and pavilions. In modern real estate terms, the Baths of Caracalla were a mixed-use entertainment and retail development.

About 1,600 bathers could use the aquatic facilities at any one time, leading scholars to believe that the complex served a total of as many as 8,000 users per day. They moved among great halls, corridors, and chambers decorated with inlaid marble and painted stucco, with niches filled with sculptures depicting Greek and Roman myths. Virtually every floor surface was covered with mosaics, ranging from black and white geometric patterns to colourful, fantastical depictions of sea creatures and allegorical figures.

Bathers moved between the frigidarium, which housed four cold baths, the tepidarium, with ambient-temperature baths, and the swimming pool. From there they could access the caldarium, the domed room 36 metres in diameter, with seven hot pools. To the senators, nobility, plebs, freed men and slaves, all of whom had free access to, and commingled in, the baths, the facility was a visually dazzling, technologically marvellous pleasure palace where clean water circulated continuously, and was offered at different, consistent temperatures depending on the experience bathers were seeking. It must have seemed effortless, almost magical, for a facility to provide so many bathing options for so many people, in a building of such grand scale. Behind – or in this case, under – the scenes, in two levels of subterranean tunnels, were hundreds of metres of sewer pipes for

outgoing water, and a hypocaust heating system where incoming water from the aqueduct was heated over wood fires. The entire complex was tended by thousands of slaves and workers, and it's estimated that more than 10 tons of wood were burned daily to keep the bathwaters heated.

Also underground was a mithraeum, a ritual site associated with worship of the Eastern god Mithras, who had developed a following among the Roman elite of the second and third centuries. The mithraeum was used for sacrificing

Bathtubs in the piazza

Though the peripheral location of the Baths of Caracalla meant they did not get built over in the ensuing centuries, their decorations and precious materials were stripped and reinstalled across Rome and the rest of Italy. If you visit the lovely Piazza Farnese (see Chapter 7), set just off Campo de'Fiori in Rome's centro storico, take note of the two graceful fountains, their bases shaped like giant bathtubs. These carved Egyptian granite vessels are from the Baths of Caracalla, where they were once used – as giant bathtubs.

Mosaic at the ruins of the Baths of Caracalla.

bulls, whose blood would pour down on worshippers below.

Caracalla never visited the bath complex that bears his name. In 217, he was killed by one of his own soldiers. The baths remained in operation until 537, when invading Goths cut off the city's water supply. The area around the baths fell out of use – too far from the city centre to be useful to a dwindling population. This physical location saved the Baths of Caracalla from complete destruction or, as was so often the case in Rome, incorporation into later structures. They were, however, used as a quarry – even the finely carved marble statues that once looked down on bathers were reduced to lime. An earthquake in 847 did major damage to the complex and it was never restored. By the mid-1500s, spoliage excavations had stripped the baths of any remaining marble, bronze and statuary. Well into the 1800s, excavations ostensibly aimed at archaeological investigation, resulted in the baths' treasures being carted away, as often as not to the Vatican Museums.

Despite the long centuries of degradation, the Baths of Caracalla remain one of Rome's most impressive archaeological sites. Surrounded by a

large open space dotted with umbrella pines, the baths are one of the few sites where modern visitors can really grasp the scale of the original complex. Still standing are several two-storey sections of brick walls, which convey the height and bulky massiveness of the structure. Remarkably intact are several large sections of the mosaic floors which once covered the entire interior pavement. Access to the underground tunnels includes the mithraeum, and exhibits that explain the hypocaust and other hydraulic workings.

While the Baths of Diocletian, inaugurated around 305, were larger than the Baths of Caracalla and could hold more bathers, they never rivalled the grandness and ornamentation of the latter. Like his predecessor 100 years before him, Diocletian ruled over an empire whose decline had already begun. With the menace of foreign marauders, the toll of internecine struggles for the emperorship, the erosion of traditional beliefs among the populace, and Diocletian's move to divide the Empire into Western and Eastern halves, Rome was ripe for change. It came in many forms – most significantly for its architectural landscape, in the worship of a new god: Jesus Christ.

HOW TO SEE IT: The Baths of Caracalla complex is about 5 minutes' walk from the Circus Maximus (Circo Massimo) Metro stop, and is open daily from 9 am to dusk (Mondays to 2 pm). For more information, visit **https://www. coopculture.it/en/heritage.cfm?id=6.**

5

CHRISTIANITY TAKES HOLD

Old St Peter's Basilica, Santa Sabina and San Saba

Roman magistrate Pontius Pilate attempted to squelch an upstart religious cult when he – by some accounts, reluctantly – ordered Christ's crucifixion in Jerusalem sometime around 33 CE. But as the story of Christ's suffering and martyrdom drew followers to him posthumously, an empire well connected by roads and shipping channels made it easier for his disciples to spread his teachings, through their own travels, through clandestine meetings and through the sharing of written versions of his works.

Throughout the Empire, there were always great disparities between rich and poor, slaves, plebs and ruling class, and human suffering was markedly higher the lower one's social status. So Christian doctrines of charity and compassion for the sick and the poor, the rejection of material trappings and the possibility of eternal salvation, regardless of caste, found a ready audience in the putrid Roman slums and among its rural, impoverished tenant farmers.

For Roman emperors and upper classes, outnumbered by millions of disaffected subjects, an emboldened populace was an unmitigated threat. And while Rome was generally tolerant of different religions and even willing to adopt some foreign gods, it always required that Roman emperors be worshipped along with these other gods. Christians, by refusing to worship, make offerings to or accept the divinity of the emperor, were considered treasonous, a danger to the legitimacy of the entire socio-political structure of the empire.

At least from the beginning of the reign of Nero in 64 CE, Christians were intermittently persecuted in Rome and throughout the Empire. Diocletian is recorded as the most ruthless and

The Dream of Constantine, from a 9th C manuscript.
Bibliothèque nationale de France/public domain

The Chi Ro, an early symbol of Christianity.

enthusiastic oppressor. During his reign (284–305) and immediately following, Christian buildings and homes were razed, and hundreds of thousands of Christians were executed, often in brutal public spectacles. Diocletian's successor, Galerius, continued the persecutions until 311, when a policy of tolerance was adopted.

The period of transition from persecution to tolerance to adoption of Christianity took place during decades of division and unrest within the empire. Not only was it divided between eastern and western halves, the Roman Empire was also governed by the Tetrarchy. This four-way power-sharing scheme, initiated by Diocletian as a means of preserving the empire, quickly descended into intrigues, power struggles and ultimately, open warfare.

In October 312, Constantine won a decisive victory at the Battle of the Milvian Bridge in Rome and took control of the Western Empire. Historical accounts and liberal doses of poetic licence recall that either the day or night before the battle, Constantine had a dream or vision of the sun with a cross above it. Other accounts claim that Constantine saw the Chi-Rho symbol, the Latin cross with its upper point in the form of a P – an early symbol for Christ. He also saw the words, *in hoc signo vinces* (in this sign, you will conquer), and reportedly had the shields of his infantrymen painted with the Chi-Rho – making them the first army to march under the protection of the Christian god.

Constantine's victory at the Milvian Bridge the next day affirmed his faith, even if he himself reportedly did not convert to Christianity until his deathbed. The Edict of Milan was declared just a few months later. It decriminalised Christianity and set in motion the transition to Christianity as the official religion of Rome.

Old St Peter's Basilica

Constantine, whether an avowed Christian or not, saw himself as emperor of the Christian people, who were now free to worship publicly, build churches and hold public office. He became a patron of the church, and sponsored the construction of church buildings throughout the empire. In Rome, his greatest building legacy would be what is now known as Old St Peter's Basilica.

Sometime between 318 and 322, Constantine ordered the construction of a basilica over the Circus of Nero, the arena and racecourse where the martyrdom of Peter the Apostle is said to have occurred more than 250 years earlier, during the reign of Nero. By the second century, the circus was no longer in use and the site was used as a necropolis. Even in the decades when Christianity was outlawed in Rome, the location where Peter was crucified contained a small shrine and was a site of veneration. Its location determined the design of the fourth-century basilica as well as that of the sixteenth-century version that stands there today.

The original church followed some aspects of the Roman basilica plan,

Plan of the Circus of Nero, with the footprint of Old St Peter's in black and the dotted outline the current basilica.

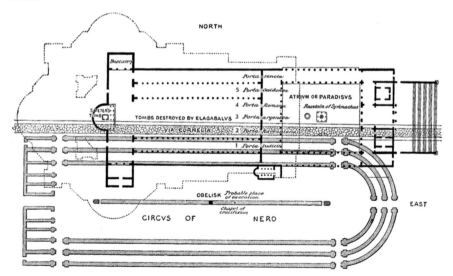

which was so effective for assembling large groups of people under one roof. Like the Basilica Julia on the Roman Forum, St Peter's featured a 110-metre long central nave with a lofty ceiling and two aisles on either side. Visitors to the basilica entered through a narthex, a covered area similar to the Roman portico. In a departure from the basilica plan, it also used the form of the Latin cross, with the nave forming the long end of the cross. The crossing, or the intersection of the transept (the short span of the cross) with the nave, formed the focal point of worship in the church, as it was the location of the raised altar and the remains of St Peter. In the apse, or semi-circular area behind the altar, a mosaic depicted Constantine and St Peter presenting a model of the church to Christ.

When it was completed about thirty years after construction began, the basilica could hold 3,000–4,000 worshippers at a time. While the exterior of the basilica was of fairly unadorned brick, the interior was ornate at every turn, with mosaics, frescoes and marble columns illuminated by tall clerestory windows in the nave and transept. The basilica was the site of papal coronations, and the most important pilgrimage destination in Europe. Wealthy pilgrims brought offerings of statuary, artwork and jewel-encrusted reliquaries, and by the ninth century, the basilica was overflowing with treasures. Papal tombs and altars, each more

Follow the Graffiti to Peter's Tomb

The tour of the archaeological excavation, or scavi, under St Peter's Basilica leads visitors to what the Catholic Church reasonably believes is the tomb containing the bones of Peter the Apostle. Researchers have pieced together evidence of the layout of the Roman-era necropolis where Peter was buried and, based on historical accounts and the results of years of excavations, have found the street of the necropolis, and even the stairs leading to Peter's tomb. A big piece of circumstantial evidence is the ancient graffiti on the walls of the necropolis, including the Chi-Ro sign, that seems to point the faithful in the direction of Peter's tomb. In the vicinity, they've even found a wall fragment with the inscription, Petros eni, which means 'Peter is here'. A small glass box filled with bones, said to be Peter's, is tucked in a wall niche. While there may never be a way to definitively prove the bones' provenance, there is convincing evidence that since the earliest days of Christian worship, the site has been venerated as Peter's Tomb.

elaborate than the next, were added to the perimeters of the aisles. In 800 CE, Charlemagne was crowned emperor of the Holy Roman Empire at St Peter's.

The safety and security once assured by the Roman Empire had long since vanished, and Rome was frequently and catastrophically menaced by foreign invaders. In 846, Saracens sacked the basilica and stripped it of much of its riches. Despite various efforts to repair St Peter's over the centuries, by the 1400s it was in such terrible condition that it was at risk of collapsing. Pope Julius II, who served from 1503 to 1513, ordered the basilica – henceforth 'Old' St Peter's – to be torn down and a new one built in its place.

Today, there are scant remains of the original St Peter's, though the focal point of the church remains the tomb of Peter, now under a grand bronze baldacchino, or pavilion, designed by Bernini. Eight of the original twelve Solomonic, or corkscrew-style columns that Constantine brought back from an Eastern temple, are now set in the four piers that support St Peter's massive dome. In the grotto of St Peter's, traces of the pre-sixteenth-century foundations can be seen, as can a glimpse of what is allegedly Peter's Tomb. In order to see parts of the original basilica, mosaicked and frescoed tombs from the late Roman necropolis, and to get close to the tomb believed to be that of the Apostle Peter, visitors must arrange in advance to tour the scavi, or archaeological excavations (see information below). For the devout, a tour of the underground scavi is a visit to one of the most revered and historically significant places in all Christendom. And regardless of one's religious convictions, the scavi tour offers a captivating history lesson and a chance to glimpse a tangible, hidden and vitally important piece of Rome's past.

Baldachin with two pairs of original Solomonic columns set in the piers on either side.
Bengt Nyman/CC2.0/Wikimedia Commons.

HOW TO SEE IT: What remains of Old St Peter's is accessed by visiting new St Peter's Basilica. Entrance to the church and grotto are free. As with all churches in Rome, proper dress is required, meaning no shorts or skirts above the knee, no bare shoulders or tank tops, and no hats. The basilica is open every day from 7 am to 7 pm in summer, and to 6 pm from October to March. See **http://www. vaticanstate.va/content/vaticanstate/ en/informazioni-utili.html** for more information. To visit the scavi and St Peter's Tomb, reserve tickets at **http:// www.scavi.va/content/scavi/en.html**. The tour currently costs €13 per person and lasts about thirty minutes.

Santa Sabina

To appreciate what the original version of St Peter's Basilica looked like, journey to the Aventine Hill and visit the Basilica of Santa Sabina. The church, now the mother church and headquarters of the Dominican Order, was built between 422 and 432, near the site of a Temple of Juno, on a high point of land overlooking the Circus Maximus and the Tiber River. Some accounts maintain that the church was built over the home of Sabina, a wealthy Roman woman martyred in the first or second century because she converted to Christianity. Another credible hypothesis doesn't concern

Exterior of Santa Sabina with nave, clerestory windows and rounded apse.
Dnalor 01/CC3.0/Wikimedia Commons

martyrdom; because Christians first worshipped secretly in private homes, it is thought that the church was simply built over the home – of a woman named Sabina – where early services took place in the first centuries after Christ. As Christians were at last free to worship in large, organised groups, it was one of about two-dozen titular churches built in Rome in the fifth century, so named because they were built over privately owned places of worship and took the name, or title, of the owner of the building.

As Christianity transitioned from being an outlawed cult to being the state religion of Rome, it was essential that it appeared stately and omnipotent, and that it crushed the remnants of

Interior of Santa Sabina, with Corinthian columns from the temple of Juno

Detail of a Corinthian column from the former pagan temple of Juno.

preserved early Christian church in Rome and provides a clear model for other churches of its era. The church follows the Roman basilica plan, but begins a period of transition between the typical basilica design of a long, central nave flanked by aisles, and later Christian churches in the form of the Latin cross. Whereas Santa Sabina did not have a transept like Old St Peter's, it departed from the basilica plan in that it had only one aisle running along either side of the nave. The clerestory, with its rows of windows set above the nave, is supported by twenty-four Corinthian marble columns from the former temple

paganism. Adopting the basilica plan transferred the symbol of Roman authority to the Christian church, and permitted thousands of worshippers to assemble in a space that simultaneously represented the protective embrace of Christ and the might of the church. Placing the church over or near a site of pagan worship – as was so often the practice throughout the early Christian world – was the literal and figurative annihilation of the pagan gods.

Santa Sabina was one of several similar churches in Rome when it was constructed, but today it is one-of-a-kind, in the sense that it is the best

The Aventino: A bourgeois address from the start

Sabina, the wealthy Roman woman for whom Santa Sabina is named, lived in one of ancient Rome's nicest neighbourhoods, the Aventino. Houses positioned on this high promontory were set well above the fetid streets of nearby Suburra to the east. They had sweeping views of the city and countryside, fresh air, and ample space for elegant villas with gardens and follies. With the collapse of Rome, the Aventino was eventually abandoned as a residential area, and became pasture and farmland. In the nineteenth and early twentieth centuries, the Aventino once again became a desirable neighbourhood, and elegant Art Deco villas and apartment buildings sprang up across the hill. Today, as in ancient times, it is considered one of the nicest addresses in Rome.

Original wooden door panel at Santa Sabina, with one of the earliest depictions of the Crucifixion of Christ. Peter1936F/CC4.0/Wikimedia Commons

of Juno – spoliage that was both practical, and symbolic of the church's dominance over the pagan past. The interior of the church, now relatively unadorned, was once lined with gold and multi-coloured mosaics, which would have reflected the light beaming in from the tall clerestory windows. The effect was intentionally celestial – the worshipper was entering not just a building, but the light-filled domain of Christ.

Though its interior has been heavily restored through the centuries, the brick exterior of Santa Sabina looks very much like it did in the fifth century, with the long nave, clerestory windows with selenite, rather than glass, panes, and the curved apse. The wooden doors through which the church is entered are original, with eighteen carved panels still surviving. One of these, in the top-left corner of the door, is one of the earliest depictions of Christ's crucifixion. Above the doorway, the original fifth-century Latin dedication remains intact, and mentions Peter of Illyria, the priest who founded the church, and Pope Celestine I, who served from 422–432 and oversaw construction of the basilica.

Restorations of Santa Sabina occurred at various points over the centuries, but the Aventine was eventually abandoned as Rome became an increasingly lawless, disease-filled place and its population dwindled. The bell tower was added in the 900s, during which time the church was fortified with a perimeter wall and served as fortress. In 1218, the basilica was granted to the Dominican friars, who built a friary that now abuts the western end of the nave. Other than a brief period at the turn of the twentieth century, Santa Sabina has served as the mother church of the Dominican Order. Restorations in the twentieth century returned the interior to a close approximation of its early Medieval state – minus the mosaics which would have run above the nave.

HOW TO SEE IT: Santa Sabina is open daily from 8.15 am to 12.30 pm and from 3.30 to 6.00 pm, with periodic closures when Mass is being celebrated. To reach the church, you have to walk (or take a taxi) up the Aventine Hill, starting from the ESE end of Via del Circo Massimo. From there, walk up the Clivio dei Publicii, then turn right on Via di Santa Sabina. The short, steep climb will take about ten minutes.

A Secret Keyhole on the Aventino

If you've made it up to Santa Sabina, continue on less than a block to the headquarters of I Cavalieri di Malta, or the Knights of Malta, one of the few surviving orders of knights of the Crusades. On the piazza, peer through the 'secret' keyhole into the gardens of the Villa del Priorato di Malta, and onto a tunnel-like, perfectly framed view of St Peter's dome. The knights have always taken seriously their vows to protect the church, and the novelty keyhole symbolises their watchful eye. If there happens to be a long line of people waiting to peep through the keyhole, you'll understand that it's not quite such a 'secret' – but still a fun thing to do if you're already up on the Aventine.

Basilica of San Saba

A short distance from Santa Sabina, on the Piccolo Aventino, or 'Little Aventino' hill, the smaller Basilica of San Saba sits on a quiet, shady spot among residential buildings. There's been some form of house of worship on this site, said to have been the home of Silvia (later Santa Silvia), mother of Pope Gregory I ('Gregory the Great'), since at least the seventh century. Today, San Saba presents an intriguing scavenger hunt of sorts, to find the pieces of its earliest past and establish a linear sense of its complicated chronology.

The basilica was first established in 645 by monks from the monastery of Mar Saba, near the Dead Sea in what is now Israel. Fleeing Islamic invaders, they sought protection in Rome, and were granted a piece of land on the

The Basilica of San Saba.

Piccolo Aventino, where a fourth-century *domus*, or Roman house had stood. As at Santa Sabina, the existing domus was probably a private site of worship during the period when Christianity was outlawed. Its association with the mother of Gregory the Great, is harder to establish and is likely more legendary than factual.

The followers of San Sabas, a fifth-century priest and monk venerated in both the Catholic Church and the Eastern Orthodox Church, constructed a basilica in the Roman style, with a nave and single aisles. This seventh-century basilica differed from the Roman style in a distinctly Eastern way: it had a triple apse plan, or a large central apse flanked by two smaller ones. These remain part of the extant footprint of the basilica. By the 600s, San Sabas was already widely revered as a performer of miracles and a founder of several major monasteries through the Middle East, and his basilica and monastery in Rome soon became one of the most important and prosperous in the city. As an Eastern church closely linked to Constantinople, it served as an important conduit between the Eastern and Western churches.

By the tenth century, deteriorating relations between Rome and Constantinople meant that San Sabas cult fell out of favour, and possession of the monastery was granted to monks of the Order of St Benedict, who were seen as being more loyal to the papacy. They

The narthex at San Saba, with some of the earliest relics from the site.

reconstructed the church in the 900s and the basic form we see now dates to that era. By the 1100s the monastery was passed to another Benedictine sect, who undertook a renovation in 1205. It was rebuilt again in the late 1400s, but San Saba's days as an important monastery had long passed. In 1573, it was granted to the *Pontificium Collegium Germanicum et Hungaricum de Urbe*, a German-speaking seminary for Roman Catholic priests. They held it through the early twentieth century, albeit in an all-but-abandoned state.

In the early 1900s, San Saba was a little-visited monastery on a deserted hill – inside the city walls but still very much on the outskirts of Rome, but an early twentieth-century building surge in Rome meant that attention was again paid to San Saba. The monastic complex was granted to the Jesuit order in the 1930s. Serious renovation and archaeological excavations were undertaken in 1943 and again in 2010, in an attempt to return the complex to the way it would have appeared in the middle ages.

Excavations have revealed parts of the seventh century building, as well as a fourth-century aula, a nave-form assembly hall that was part of the original Roman domus. The original façade is covered by a portico, or

Cosmatesque column with Corinthian capital, San Saba.

Cosmatesque mosaic floors at San Saba.

external narthex, built in the 1400s and featuring six ancient columns pillaged from other Roman sites. The portico contains some of the oldest pieces of the site, including a carved Roman sarcophagus and other sculptural fragments. Particularly rare pieces are those that decorated the seventh-century monastery, including a relief of a knight and a falcon. From the portico, the central doorway, flanked by two blocked, arched doorways, marks the entrance to the fourth-century aula, which originally had three doors.

The nave of San Saba is supported by pillaged columns. Especially noteworthy

in the church is the well-preserved thirteenth-century *cosmatesque* flooring, a style imported from Byzantium and typified by colourful patterns of inlaid stone. The decorative style also appears on bits of door moulding and columns in the church interior. The crypt, which once housed the tomb of San Saba (his remains, brought to Rome by twelfth-century Crusaders who stole them from the Holy Land, were returned to the Mar Saba monastery in Israel in 1965 – today,

Fresco fragments at San Saba.

practices of spoliage, reincorporating old parts into new structures, filling in old structures and building on top of them make a chronological reading of the basilica all but impossible, even to the trained eye. Coupled with that, the nineteenth- and twentieth-century practice of restoring early churches by removing evidence of later renovations was often carried out in a manner that was haphazard at best. Still, the basilica complex, apart from offering a quiet, verdant space away from the crowds of central Rome, offers a tantalising glimpse of monastic architecture in the early middle ages.

HOW TO SEE IT: San Saba is on the Piccolo Aventino and is reached by heading about five minutes on foot up Via di San Saba, from where it meets Viale Aventino at the bottom of the hill. A visit here can be combined with a day spent exploring nearby Santa Sabina (1 km north-west), and the Baths of Caracalla, which are about 1 km north-east of San Saba. The basilica is open Monday through Saturday from 8 am to 12 pm and again from 4 pm to 7 pm. On Sundays, it opens at 9.30 am. Non-worshippers will not be able to enter the church when Mass is being held. The basilica's official website, **https://sansaba.gesuiti.it**, contains some helpful information but is geared toward the current activities of the Jesuit community.

only an arm bone remains) is built into the fourth-century Roman domus.

For modern visitors, San Saba presents the very complicated nature of parsing the architecture of Rome in the early Middle Ages. The widespread

THE MIDDLE AGES

The Basilicas of Santa Maria in Trastevere, San Clemente & San Nicola in Carcere

By the high Middle Ages, the period generally defined as 1000–1300, Rome's population had fallen from as much as one million during the Empire to a mere 30,000 living within the third-century Aurelian walls. Crumbling ancient monuments, including the hulks of the Colosseum, the Baths of Caracalla and the ruins of the Forum dotted the cityscape. Defensive towers constructed by rival and often warring families poked out from what would have appeared as an otherwise low-rise – and surprisingly pastoral – panorama. With the lack of a consistently functioning central government, residents organised themselves into village-like neighbourhoods, usually built around a titular church, basilica or monastery, and especially close to the Tiber, the only source of water since the aqueducts had long since been destroyed.

While control of the city had ostensibly belonged to the papacy since the 600s, the centuries after the fall of Rome were marked by frequent, violent clashes for claim to the Papal throne and catastrophic sackings of the city. During periods of relative stability, building projects were undertaken, either sponsored by the church or a wealthy patron, but never at the pace or scale of the Roman Empire, or even with the frequency and ambition of the dozens of titular churches built during the early days of Christian Rome.

Rome has been called a city nearly devoid of Medieval architecture, and the cityscape does appear to leap directly from classical monuments to Renaissance structures. Understanding this gap in the architectural timeline means jumping forward to the fifteenth-century Renaissance era, when Europe emerged from the so-called 'Dark Ages' and entered a period of intellectual and creative growth that was likened to the glory days of the Empire. As a result, buildings constructed after the fall of Rome and well into the late Middle

Ages were considered representative of unenlightened times. As the architects of the Renaissance looked to the elegant symmetrical designs and engineering marvels of their ancient Roman predecessors, the often clumsy, utilitarian buildings of the Middle Ages were pulled down, replaced with new structures that reflected the grandeur of Ancient Rome.

Further destruction of Rome's Medieval past occurred in the late nineteenth century, with the construction of the Vittoriano (see Chapter 9), the monument to Vittorio Emanuele II, the first king of unified Italy. Building the massive structure, now a major landmark in Rome, meant wiping out an entire Medieval neighbourhood, including several churches, at the base of the Capitoline Hill. Via dei Fori Imperiali, built by Mussolini in the 1920s and 30s, cut a swath across more of Medieval Rome and levelled buildings dating from the ninth century onwards.

As a result, buildings that preserve the true character of the high Middle Ages are rare in Rome, and are primarily churches. And as seen in Chapter 5, there are virtually no examples of a 'pure' form of Medieval architecture in Rome. From the fall of the Empire up to (and to an extent, including) the Renaissance, the practice of spoliage laid waste to Rome's ancient monuments. The use of old building parts to construct new buildings was the symbolic triumph over the pagan past,

as well as an exercise in trophy-hunting. But it was also very much a custom of necessity – it was simply cheaper and easier to use existing materials like iron, marble and brick than it was to forge, carve or pour new ones. So just as there are few early Christian buildings that aren't held up – at least in part – by Classical columns, there are no extant buildings from the high Middle Ages that don't bear evidence of layers of construction, spoliage and restoration, and the liberal mixing of styles of different epochs.

Santa Maria in Trastevere

If you could walk around the perimeter of the Basilica of Santa Maria in Trastevere, you'd see a building that looks very much like a smaller version of Old St Peter's – a Roman basilica plan with a central nave and aisles, a transept forming a modified Latin cross, and a semi-circular apse. Today, the church and the piazza in front of it are the heart of Trastevere, one of Rome's oldest and most colourful neighbourhoods.

While the basilica may have once been a freestanding building in the midst of a working-class Rome suburb, it's now tucked tightly into a dense warren of medieval – and in some cases, older – buildings. Though few traces of the original basilica remain, the Santa Maria in Trastevere is a remarkable study in how an early church evolved through remodels and restorations, and it's a case study in how Papal spoliage

Santa Maria in Trastevere.

stripped ancient Roman monuments of their valuable materials in order to create and enhance churches that are now themselves part of Rome's cultural patrimony.

Most of the current Santa Maria in Trastevere dates from a twelfth-century renovation under the direction of Pope Innocent II, who most likely came from a family of the Trastevere district. However, this has been a place of worship since as early as 220 CE,

when Pope Callixtus dedicated a titular church here, at a site thought to be near his home. By the mid-fifth century the church was dedicated by Pope Celestine to the Virgin Mary, making it one of the oldest – if not the oldest – churches in Rome in her honour.

Between Santa Maria in Trastevere's founding in the third century and the current build from the twelfth century, it had been damaged and restored several times, including after the 410

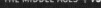

Getting lost in Trastevere

Despite it no longer being an 'undiscovered' enclave outside of Rome's centro storico, Trastevere (the name means 'across the river') retains its outsider appeal and, most charmingly, its Medieval character. Streets here follow the narrow paths they've wound since at least the early Middle Ages. There's been a fountain at the centre of Piazza di Santa Maria in Trastevere since the age of Augustus and today, the buzzing piazza is still very much the heart of the neighbourhood. At night, the basilica's gold mosaics are floodlit to a dreamy glow. Still, I encourage you to explore the winding streets leading off from the piazza, where you'll find fewer crowds, cosy little trattorias and simple bars, and a true sense of a real Roman neighbourhood.

so was the extensive and elaborate rebuilding of the basilica in Trastevere, one of the few vanity projects he was able to realise during his troubled tenure.

A 12th century mosaic from Santa Maria in Trastevere, with Pope Innocent II holding a model of the church.

Sack of Rome by the Visigoths. In 1140, when Pope Innocent II ordered a major renovation of Santa Maria in Trastevere, most of the church was demolished, though the approximate footprint of the structure was retained.

Innocent II's thirteen-year papacy was tumultuous, with a Papal schism dominating more than half of it. With a rival 'antipope' laying claim to the Holy See, Innocent struggled to prove his power and efficacy. One means of doing

Marble columns in Santa Maria in Trastevere, some of which are known to have come from the Baths of Caracalla.

Scholars know that materials used in Santa Maria's Middle Ages reconstruction were taken from buildings dating from the Roman empire, but determining which spolia was sourced from where – and which were indeed 'new' in 1140 – is more challenging. Of eighteen pre-medieval column capitals lining either side of the

Twelfth-century apse mosaic at Santa Maria in Trastevere depicting the Coronation of the Virgin.
Gary Campbell-Hall/CC2.0.

nave, eight – depicting pagan gods that would have been unknown iconography to medieval viewers – are confirmed as from the Baths of Caracalla. Others may be from a first- or second–century Temple of Isis on the nearby Janiculum Hill. In total there are twenty-two granite columns in the nave, of ancient Roman provenance but with their specific source unknown.

Most aspects of the new church were added during the twelfth-century rebuild, including several exquisite mosaics on the interior and exterior of the church. The golden apse mosaic depicts the Coronation of the Virgin, with a seated Mary enthroned next to Christ. The figure on the far left, clad in red and white robes, is Innocent himself, presenting a model of the church to the holy family. The ornate coffered ceiling is from a seventeenth-century restoration.

The exterior of the church still bears twelfth- and thirteenth-century gold mosaics, including a procession of saints venerating Mary. Below the mosaics, the walls of a nineteenth-century portico – probably built to replace a crumbling predecessor – are embedded with dozens of paleo-Christian inscriptions

Exterior of Santa Maria Trastevere, with 12th- and 13th-century mosaics. Bjsamelsonjones/Public domain.

from the earliest phases of the basilica. Captivating as they are to observe under the portico, they illustrate the haphazard manner in which previous excavations and renovations were carried out, with ancient inscriptions, architectural elements and sarcophagi regarded as random treasure, rather than for their scientific or historic value.

Roman and early Christian epigraphs in the portico of Santa Maria in Trastevere. Sailko/CC3.0/Wikimedia Commons.

HOW TO SEE IT: The basilica is open daily from 7.30 am to 12 pm, and again from 4 pm to 9 pm. Entrance is free.

Basilica of Saint Clemente

Perhaps more than any other church in Rome, the Basilica of San Clemente (officially the Basilica di San Clemente in Laterano) demonstrates Rome's proclivity for repurposing ancient structures. The church is dedicated to Pope St Clement, who was either the second or third Bishop of Rome – the equivalent of Pope – after St Peter. Clement was executed sometime around 100 CE, under the reign of Trajan, by being tied to an anchor and tossed into the Black Sea. (He is now the patron saint of mariners.) His remains were recovered and brought back to Rome, though his skull purportedly rests in the Kiev Monastery of the Caves in Ukraine, near the site of his martyrdom.

Unlike many churches in Rome, San Clemente offers a nearly linear study in how structures were built on top of one another. It is generally divided into three layers, though in fact each of those layers has several builds and rebuilds on the same foundation. The original building, which might have been a warehouse, dates to the mid- to late-

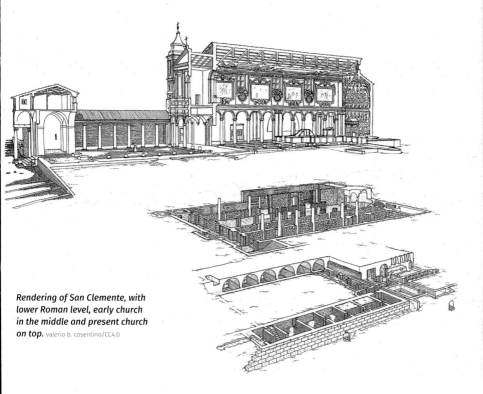

Rendering of San Clemente, with lower Roman level, early church in the middle and present church on top. valerio b. cosentino/CC4.0

The Mithreum in the lower level of San Clemente.
Allie Caulfield/CC2.0

Roman Republic, and was destroyed in the Great Fire of 64 CE. An apartment building, or insula, was built on top of this ruined structure, as was a grander home belonging to Titus Flavius Clemens – considered by many scholars to be the same person as the future St Clement. Evidence suggests it was a clandestine Christian meeting place in the late first century, which would be consistent with the space later being used for a titular church. With the resurgence of the cult of Mithras in the second and third centuries CE, the courtyard of the apartment, or insula, was used as a Mithraeum, a space for bull sacrifices associated with the rites of the Eastern deity.

Over these Roman structures, the first Basilica of San Clemente was built sometime in the early fourth century, though its exact date of construction is unknown. This basilica was actively maintained and upgraded through the eleventh century. In the early twelfth century, a second basilica – the present one – was built on top of the Roman and early-Christian structures, which laid buried until the 1800s, when excavations began to reveal San Clemente's past. Today, a visit to the archaeological area under the present basilica offers one of the best places in Rome to understand the practice of filling in ancient structures to make new ones, and of the repurposing of old buildings.

The church was restored in the 1700s, its interior – in particular the elaborate gilded and frescoed ceiling – was largely refashioned in the Baroque style. Still, the present church features an exceptionally noteworthy collection of Middle Ages art, decor, and relics. Its floorplan still follows the traditional basilica form of a long nave and aisles

Floor mosaics from the fourth-century church of San Clemente. Palickap/CC4.0.

Nave and apse of the 12th-century, upper church of San Clemente. Sixtus/CC3.0.

capped by an apse, with later chapels added along the aisles. The restored cosmatesque mosaic floor dates from the 1100s, while the marble choir box near the front of the nave is original to the church below, and dates from the sixth century. When the basilica below San Clemente was filled in with rubble, this schola cantorum was saved and reassembled in the new building. Roman spolia columns separate the current nave from the aisles. Much of the altar dates from the seventeenth-century restoration, though the stone awning dates from the Middle Ages, and the throne behind the altar is from the lower basilica.

Underground, further extensive evidence of the first basilica still exists, including frescoes lining the nave

The entrance to the Basilica of San Clemente.
Nicholas Frisardi/CC2.0.

HOW TO SEE IT: The easy-to-miss entrance to the basilica is on Via San Giovanni in Laterano, a 5-minute walk east of the Colosseum. It's open Monday to Saturday from 9 am to 12.30 pm, and again from 3 pm to 6 pm, and on Sundays from 12–5.30 pm. Entrance to the church is free, but a self-guided tour of the underground costs €10 per person. Photos are not permitted in the excavations, and visitors are required to dress modestly, as they would to visit a church.

An underground river

At almost any point of the underground tour of San Clemente, you'll hear the sound of rushing water. And in a few places, you can see the subterranean river that's part of the Cloaca Maxima, the underground sewer system built in the sixth century BCE and that eventually empties into the Tiber. For more on this ancient Roman sanitation system, see Chapter 2.

and dating from the ninth to eleventh centuries, making them among the oldest and best-preserved Christian imagery in Rome. The length of the first nave is open, and visitors can see the Mithraeum and rooms of the Roman houses. Take note, though, of the staircases and doors that are sealed off with brick or stone, evidence that there are potentially many more rooms and spaces to be excavated.

In comparison to its rich interiors and atmospheric underground levels, the exterior of San Clemente is restrained to the point of banality. It's hemmed in by a windowless wall, and entered through a Baroque-era side door with minimal signage. The original entrance to the basilica at the short end of the nave is slightly below street level but is now closed. Unlike the elaborate facades of the Renaissance and Baroque churches that would come after it, San Clemente keeps its treasures hidden on the inside.

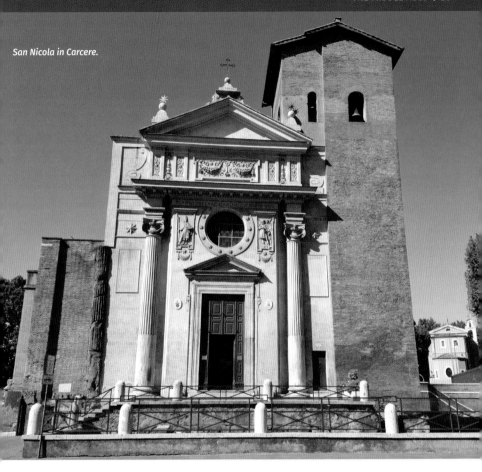

San Nicola in Carcere.

San Nicola in Carcere

The name San Nicola in Carcere translates to 'Saint Nicolas in Prison', suggesting a straightforward story of a Christian saint once imprisoned on the site of this church west of the Capitoline Hill. But the etymology of this mostly eleventh-century church is far from clear, since there is no reliable means of dating the church to prior to 1088. Scholars surmise that one of the three Roman-era temples on which the church is built may have served as a prison during the fifth or sixth century. It's also possible that a prison was nearby, and the term came to refer to the entire area. San Nicola – the same St Nick of Santa Claus fame – lived during the third and fourth century and by the seventh century was widely venerated in the Eastern Orthodox church. His relics were stolen from Myra, in present-day Turkey,

Southern façade of San Nicola in Carcere, with columns from the Temple of Spes. Berthold Werner/CC3.0.

and brought to Bari, Italy, in 1087, after which time his cult of worship became widespread. There is no evidence that he ever set foot in Rome or has other associations with titular basilica in Rome that bears his name.

Much like the Basilica of San Clemente – though not nearly as neatly vertically oriented – San Nicola in Carcere is built upon the ruins of three Republican-era temples, at the site of the former Forum Horitorium, a produce market where fruits and

vegetables were sold. In the typical practice of adaptive reuse, the temples were incorporated throughout the basilica, most obviously on its exterior; its façade contains two fluted ionic columns from the second-century BCE Temple of Juno Sospita. The left, or southern exterior wall of the church (if looking at the front of the church), incorporates six columns from the third-century BCE Temple of Spes. Built into the right/northern exterior wall are columns belonging to the former Temple of Janus. The bell tower, however, dates from the thirteenth century.

Though a Christian place of worship

may have been sited over at least one of the temples as early as the 500s, the earliest reliable dating suggests that the present footprint of the basilica dates to the eleventh century, when it was built or rebuilt under the supervision of Pope Urban II. For the next 500 years, the church went through a series of redesigns and restructurings, as well as different names. It was known briefly as San Nicola Petrus Leonis, during which time a Cosmatesque patterned floor and choir stall were added. Both the floor and the schola cantorum have been remarkable well preserved, despite the frequent structural and interior renovations.

In 1599, the church was again rebuilt and the present façade was added. It was renovated several times in the 1800s, but barely survived Mussolini's city planning – note the hulking Fascist-

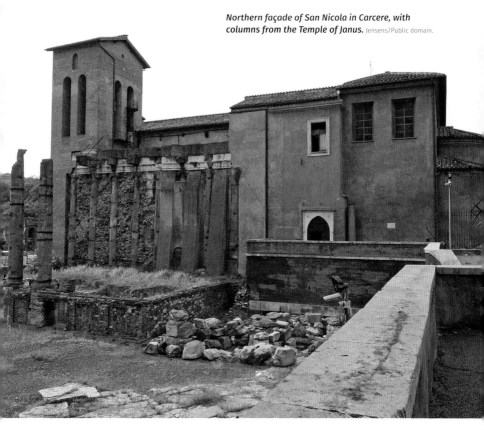

Northern façade of San Nicola in Carcere, with columns from the Temple of Janus. Jensens/Public domain.

Nave of San Nicola in Carcere, with mismatched columns of various origin. Luc./CC1.0.

era government complex right next door – which levelled the Medieval residential area around the basilica and resulted in the neighbourhood being depopulated.

Archaeologists believe that the original basilica – from the sixth century or later – incorporated the main Temple of Juno by using its columns to delineate the nave from the aisles and support the clerestory above the nave. The exterior walls of the original basilica were formed by the northern row of columns from the Temple of Spes and the southern row of columns of the Temple of Janus, which were filled in with brick to make solid walls. This theory does not explain, however, why the nave is formed by a mismatched pastiche of fluted and smooth, Corinthian and Ionic columns which clearly didn't originate in a single temple. One theory is that the temple was in such a state of disrepair by the Middle Ages that the original columns would not have had the structural

Republican temple foundations underneath the present San Nicola in Carcere. Lalupa/CC3.0.

integrity to support the new church, and other spolia was utilised.

Under the altar, modern visitors can access the crypt containing the foundations of the three temples. Between the column podiums of the central temple of Juno Sospita and northern temple of Janus, a piece of the ancient road that ran through the Forum Horitorium has been uncovered. Also located in this room are several large square chambers, the exact purpose of which are unknown, and a small chapel, thought to be from the 600s. Like the temples of Portunus and Hercules Victor, their much-better preserved

contemporaries down the road, these temple remnants represent some of the oldest Republican-era ruins in the city.

HOW TO SEE IT: San Nicola in Carcere is open daily from 10 am to 5 pm. The archaeological area in the crypt has the same hours, but is closed on Wednesdays. Access to the crypt is by guided tour only, after which a donation is expected.

RENAISSANCE ROME

Santa Maria del Popolo, Palazzo Farnese, Villa Medici

A series of events over decades and centuries helped create the foundation for the cultural flowering in Europe that would become known as the Renaissance. In northern Europe, the unsparing devastation of the Black Death in the mid-1300s eroded faith in God and the Catholic church, and laid the groundwork for the intellectual and spiritual revolutions that characterised the Northern Renaissance. But in Italy, it was largely the growth, not the weakening, of the church that fomented the Italian Renaissance. For the papacy, the definitive fall of Constantinople and the Eastern Roman Empire to the Ottomans in 1453 was a turning point.

The Catholic church was now the unrivalled spiritual voice of the Christian world, and Rome was once again its epicentre of political power, financial resources and military might. This ushered in a period of both secular and non-secular building that was unprecedented since Imperial Rome. Rival city Florence may have been the artistic hub of the Italian Renaissance, but for architectural achievements, Rome was its centre.

In Rome, the epoch of grand public architecture, in the form of temples and basilicas, had long ago ebbed with the Empire. But the desire for grandiosity remained, and the means for realising epic building works were in the hands of either the popes or wealthy, noble families, most of whom had Papal connections or ambitions. In place of public architecture came new and completely renovated churches, and ostentatious private palaces and villas.

As Italy and all of Europe emerged from the 'dark' centuries of the Medieval era, Rome was a city desperately in need of a facelift. Its population had dwindled; its churches and basilicas had fallen into disrepair and its ancient monuments had been pillaged for *spolia* or pulled down during periods of violent invasions. Architecturally, the new 'kings' of Rome – the Popes – and the artists who carried out their bidding did much like Mussolini would do five centuries later; they looked to the peak period of the Roman Empire for the inspiration to remake Rome. The ancient principles of order and symmetry, and the resilient elements of arches, domes and columns were all rediscovered and reconsidered during this period, as the artists and architects whose legacies were born in the Renaissance sought to take the lessons of Imperial Rome and apply them to the age in which they lived.

Santa Maria del Popolo

Unlike many churches in Rome whose origins are documented often as far back as antiquity, the Basilica of Santa Maria del Popolo starts sometime in the eleventh century, with a myth. According to writings dating from the fifteenth century, the basilica stands at the spot, now on the Piazza del Popolo, where Emperor Nero was buried. A tree grew from his bones, and was supposedly inhabited by otherworldly creatures – said to be demons, anti-Christian spirits or even the ghost of Nero himself. The tomb was near the Porta Flaminia, one of the main points of entry into the city, and the tree was said to attack travellers – who would have been many – passing through the area. Pope Paschal II, who reigned from 1099 to 1118, led an exorcism of the tree, which was then removed. The stone set in its

Petrarch's Pejorative

This sleep of forgetfulness will not last forever. – Petrarch

Fourteenth-century scholar and poet Petrarch (1304–1374) took a dim view of the age in which he lived, to the point that he is credited with introducing the term 'Dark Ages' to refer to the period from the fall of Rome to the birth of the Renaissance in the mid-15th century. While the term is no longer used among scholars to describe the period, the association has been hard to shake. Petrarch's writings contrast the periods of Greek and Roman Antiquity as ones of cultural and intellectual enlightenment versus the period after the fall of Rome as one of cultural stagnation and human degradation and suffering. Given that Petrarch lived through the 1347–48 outbreak of the Bubonic Plague, one of the most climatic and catastrophic events of the Middle Ages, perhaps it's no surprise that he had such a pessimistic view of the human condition.

place allegedly became the first stone of the altar of the church that would later become Santa Maria del Popolo.

The name *del popolo* – 'of the people' – may come from the belief that Paschal delivered the people of Rome from the evil scourge of the tree, or, more simply, may be derived from

Basilica di Santa Maria del Popolo.
Picture by M0tty/CC3.0

the poplar trees that were said to have grown in the area. Research indicates that Nero was not buried on this spot. And the menacing tree of Medieval lore was more likely the bandits of the area, who lay in wait – perhaps hidden in trees – ready to ambush hapless travellers entering or leaving the city. Still, the basilica grew in importance as a pilgrimage church.

Francesco della Rovere assumed the papacy in 1471 as Sixtus IV, and quickly positioned himself as the rebuilder of Rome. His papacy marks a clear flowering of the Roman-Papal Renaissance, as he brought to the city painters, sculptors and architects with the intention of securing his legacy and establishing Rome once and for all as the spiritual and intellectual centre of Europe. When he became pontiff, he ordered a complete rebuilding of the basilica, which is the current structure still seen today. The medieval church, of which very little is known, was completely demolished. The church that went up in its place is still considered a prototype for early Renaissance architecture.

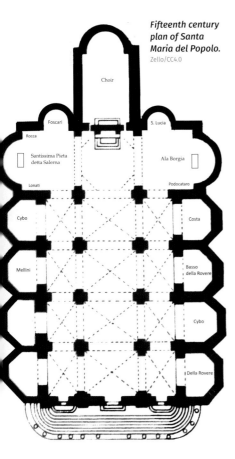

Fifteenth century plan of Santa Maria del Popolo.
Zello/CC4.0

Two smaller entrances flank a central, main entrance, much like the three entrances that once led to the cellae of the Temple of Jupiter Optimus Maximus on the Capitoline Hill. The four pilasters, or false columns topped by Corinthian capitals, and the three false pediments over the doors have no structural function but instead pay homage to their Imperial counterparts.

Inside, the floorplan follows that of a Roman basilica and subsequent Christian structures: a central nave with an aisle on either side and an apse at one end. The aisles are delineated with pillars formed of engaged columns surmounted by arches. The basilica is in the form of a Latin cross, with a dome over the crossing of the nave and transept. The octagonal dome – the first to be built in Rome since Antiquity – served as a precursor to the more elegant and architecturally complex domes that would rise during the Renaissance. The choir, added to the apse between 1505 and 1510, was designed by Renaissance master architect Donato Bramante, once contained paintings by Raphael and features some of the oldest stained glass windows in Rome.

Though firmly fixed in its epoch, a quick study of the façade of Santa Maria del Popolo reveals just how carefully Renaissance architects were studying the works of their Roman predecessors. The basilica's façade is restrained, nearly flat and geometrically precise, with traits that harken back to Rome's earliest temples, beginning at the stairs that lead up the podium to its doors.

As Sixtus IV, his successors and his cohorts, many of whom were his nephews, increasingly administered the papacy like a monarchy, they, like the emperors of Rome, had motives to present shows of grandiosity. Santa Maria del Popolo provides examples

Octagonal dome of Santa Maria del Popolo.

of this Papal propaganda in its side chapels, which were purchased by cardinals – and sometimes by future Popes – to serve as elaborately decorated tombs. The chapels of Santa Maria del Popolo are the vanity pieces of the Renaissance (and later, the Baroque-era) Papal families, adorned with

Dome of the Chigi Chapel, with design and mosaics by Raphael.

intricate paintings and sculptures and ostentatious tombs. Best known among them is the Chigi Chapel, designed by Raphael for Agostino Chigi, a wealthy banker. The artist is known to have looked to the Pantheon as inspiration for the ornate chapel. It also features a dome, decorated with mosaics from Raphael – the only surviving example of his work in mosaic.

While the floorplan and architectural 'bones' of Santa Maria del Popolo retain the characteristics of the Renaissance structure, much of the ornamentation

in the basilica is full-on Baroque. A renovation, begun in 1658 at the behest of Pope Alexander VII and executed by Gian Lorenzo Bernini, added the white stucco embellishments and dramatically changed the size of some windows to better control the light – a concept begun in the late Renaissance but heavily emphasised during the Baroque. Alexander VII was of the Chigi family, and oversaw the refurbishment of the Chigi Chapel to include its

Bramante's Tempietto at Chiesa di San Pietro in Montorio.

Bramante's Renaissance perfection

If you climb the stairs from Trastevere to the Janiculum Hill (Gianicolo in Italian), you'll walk past the Chiesa di San Pietro in Montorio and should by all means go inside. The church with the austere façade has a nearly riotous interior, rich with Renaissance and Baroque paintings and sculptures, including a chapel designed entirely by Bernini. But the treasure most visitors seek is outdoors, in the cloister; the Tempietto, or 'little temple' created by Donato Bramante sometime around 1502. Built on what is traditionally considered the exact spot where St Peter was martyred, the Tempietto is a small, circular tomb monument that serves no real architectural function yet is regarded as a prototype of High Renaissance architecture. Bramante studied the round Temple of Vesta at Hadrian's villa at Tivoli, outside Rome, the Pantheon, as well as the Temple of Hercules Victor at the Forum Boarium (see Chapter 2) to create the petite monument, which soon after its completion was considered the epitome of Renaissance perfection. The architectural elements most visible in the Tempietto – its dome and simplified Classical columns – combined with it symmetry, geometric perfection and restrained ornamentation, made it a model for other works in Rome and throughout Italy, including Brunelleschi's dome of the Duomo in Florence, and Bramante's own work at St Peter's Basilica.

Note that the Tempietto is in the courtyard of what is now the Spanish Academy (**www.accademiaspagna.org/**). Current visiting hours are Tuesday – Sunday from 10 am to 6 pm.

current Baroque elements.

Although the Baroque influence is heavily felt at Santa Maria del Popolo, the façade, floorplan and aspects of the interior are true to their Renaissance roots. The two artistic and architectural epochs, combined, make the basilica a treasure trove of liturgical art; in addition to the works of Raphael and sculptures and embellishments from Bernini, the basilica contains two of Caravaggio's most important paintings, the Crucifixion of St Peter and Conversion on the Way to Damascus, plus works from Pinturicchio, Annibale Carracci, and other lesser-known stars of the Renaissance and Baroque.

HOW TO SEE IT: The basilica is at the northern end of Piazza del Popolo, with the entrance just to the right of the Porta del Popolo old city gate. Visiting hours to the basilica are Monday-Friday from 7.30 am to 12.30 pm, and from 4 pm to 7 pm. Saturday hours are 7.30 am to 7 pm. On Sunday, the basilica is open from 7.30 am to 1.30 pm, and from 4.30 pm to 7 pm. For the best viewing times with the least crowds, try visiting when the basilica opens at 7.30 am, or in the evenings just before closing. The basilica is closed to visitors during Mass. Admission is free, though you will need euro coins to illuminate the Caravaggio paintings.

Palazzo Farnese

Long considered Rome's most celebrated example of High and Late Renaissance architecture, Palazzo Farnese, now the home of the Embassy of France, was first commissioned as the home of the wealthy and powerful Farnese family. It took more than seventy years to complete and as a result, Palazzo Farnese bears the influence of some of the most important architects of the sixteenth century, including Michelangelo, who oversaw one phase of its design and execution.

Construction of the Palazzo Farnese began at the behest of Cardinal Alessandro Farnese. Farnese had been named a cardinal by Pope Alexander VI, the notorious Borgia Pope whose long-time mistress, Giulia Farnese, was Alessandro's sister. For decades after Alexander VI's death in 1503, Cardinal Farnese wielded influence with successive popes and built his family's fortune. As the profile of the Farnese Family grew, they needed a palatial home that demonstrated this wealth and influence. In 1517, Alessandro Farnese commissioned Antonio de Sangallo the Younger to design the palace and oversee its construction. De Sangallo had been an assistant to Donato Bramante and was already an established architect when he undertook Palazzo Farnese. He was charged with building Rome's most magnificent palace, one befitting the princely status and lifestyle of the Farnese cardinal.

Front façade of Palazzo Farnese. Peter1936F/CC4.0

Progress on the palace was interrupted during the 1527 Sack of Rome by invading troops of Holy Roman Emperor Charles V. Rome remained in turmoil for several years and by the time Alessandro Farnese ascended to the Papal throne as Paul III in 1534, the Catholic church was dealing with a new threat in the north: the Protestant Reformation.

While the Reformation movement started by Martin Luther in 1517 would create distraction and discord in Northern Europe for more than a century, and ultimately undermine the influence of the Catholic church in the north, in Italy it had an almost opposite effect: the menace of the Reformation allowed the church to tighten its grip in Italy and achieve even greater wealth and power. Reformers in Italy were treated as heretics and dealt with swiftly and harshly, to the point that there was no real Reformation threat within the Italian peninsula.

The re-solidified wealth and power of the church in Italy extended to the personal fortunes and prestige of the Pope himself, and Paul III turned his attention to constructing Palazzo Farnese on an even grander scale. By 1545, Sangallo was still the architect of the palazzo but had apparently fallen out of favour with the Pope. In a turn of events said to have contributed to Sangallo's death the following year (though he died from malaria, rather than shame), he was replaced as lead architect by Michelangelo. However, the building was only under Michelangelo's guidance for four years, as his own deteriorating health and other projects pulled him away from the work. The design was left to Giacomo Barozzi da Vignola, who stayed mostly true to the

Palazzo Farnese in an 18th-century etching by Giuseppe Vasi.

previous designs, followed by Giacomo della Porta, who lent a late mannerist influence to the building's interiors and top floor.

Sangallo's original plans for the palace revealed a true dedication to Renaissance principles of symmetrical, yet rhythmical design, with rows of rectangular windows on the piano nobile (noble floor, in this case, the second storey) capped by alternating triangular and segmental, or curved, pediments. This symmetrical field of windows across the three floors of the palace form a harmonious grid, that gives the imposing, square-shaped building an almost monolithic appearance, interrupted only by a substantial door and balcony in the centre of the facade.

The palace was designed around a central courtyard, which Sangallo based on the front façade (no longer extant) of the Theatre of Marcellus (see Chapter 3), with its lower level of pillars engaged Doric columns, Ionic pilasters on the second level and Corinthian pilasters on the third, uppermost level.

When Michelangelo took over the direction of the palace's construction, he adhered to Sangallo's design for the first two floors, with a few notable additions, including the large architrave, or lintel, above the main door. He also added the massive Papal coat-of-arms above the balcony from which Paul III would hold public audiences on the square facing the palace – proof that Michelangelo knew how to ingratiate himself to his fickle patron. The deep, sharply angled cornice, or moulding, at the roof level is also the work of Michelangelo.

Paul III died in 1549, with

Balcony of Palazzo Farnese, with Farnese family Papal coat of arms. Jean-Pierre Dalbéra/CC2.0

the palace still incomplete. In 1550, Giacomo Barozzi da Vignola took over as chief architect, though his role was mostly to execute the existing designs of his predecessors. Palazzo Farnese's final architect, Giacomo della Porta, was responsible for many of the details added after 1570, including in the courtyard. Michelangelo's original concept for the third storey included a loggia, or covered porch, on the northeast, or piazza-side wing overlooking the courtyard that would have melded indoor and outdoor living spaces. Della Porta, instead, built the third floor as a solid, windowed wall.

On all three levels of the courtyard,

the exaggerated proportions of the engaged columns, the juxtaposition of triangular pediments set in arches along the second level, the non-structural rectangular insets on the third level

The enclosed courtyard of Palazzo Farnese.

and the presence of sculpted garlands along the architraves are the hallmarks of the Late Renaissance. Also referred to a Mannerism in art and architecture, the style is distinguished by willingness to depart from the sober harmony and symmetry of the Renaissance, for an effect that is more decorative and whimsical. Mannerism is seen as the precursor to the unbridled ornamentation of the Baroque style that would dominate in the 1600s.

With its epitomical High Renaissance façade and the interior courtyard that clearly marks the stylistic bridge between the Renaissance and the Baroque, the palazzo is also remarkable in that its architecture has been painstakingly preserved and unaltered since its completion in 1589.

HOW TO SEE IT: Filled with artistic masterpieces of the Renaissance and Baroque, Palazzo Farnese is the seat of the French Embassy in Rome and as such, is not open to the public on a walk-in basis. Instead, tours can be booked through InventerRome, the only group authorised for bookings. Tours in English are offered one day a week (currently Wednesdays) and are limited to twenty-five persons per tour. This means you'll need to reserve your visit months in advance. Tours currently cost €9 per person, and can be booked at https://www.inventerrome.com/index.php/en/.

While construction of grand buildings stretching over decades – or even centuries – was not unusual in Rome, the continuity achieved at Palazzo Farnese, despite decades of work and a handful of architects, solidifies its place as Rome's finest Renaissance building.

Villa Medici

Perhaps no family name is more connected with the Italian Renaissance than that of the Medici. The Medici, a family of bankers, were a political and religious force in Italy from the thirteenth to the eighteenth centuries, associated with everything from the rise of Papal power to the economic and political scandals that shaped the country's development for hundreds of years to follow. As a result of their direct financial support of the arts, the Medici are mentioned in the same breath as Italy's best-known artists and architects, and countless important buildings and monuments – especially in Florence – are attributed to their patronage.

The Medici dynasty figured prominently in the papacy of the sixteenth century, with three Medici serving as Popes (Leo X [1513–21], Clement VII [1523–34], and Pius IV [1559–65]), though the latter was a distant relative of the main Medici bloodline. Leo X and Clement VII, while remembered for commissioning works from the leading artists of the Renaissance, particularly Michelangelo and Raphael, also presided over and were at least partly responsible for decades of war and shifting alliances, which ultimately weakened Rome and the papacy. So it is ironic, perhaps, that the most prominent building in Rome to bear the Medici name was neither constructed during the High Renaissance nor by a Medici Pope, but decades later, when the Medici influence in Rome had already started to wane.

Villa Medici sits on the Pincian Hill,

The streetside exterior of Villa Medici.
José Luiz Bernardes Ribeiro/CC4.0

An esteemed 'prisoner'

Galileo Galilei was a friend of the Medici court, even when that friendship ran afoul of the papacy. When, in 1633, Galileo was ordered to Rome to face charges of heresy brought by the Roman Catholic Inquisition, he was a guest – under 'house arrest' – at Villa Medici. Found guilty in June of that year of 'vehement suspicion of heresy' for proposing his theory that the sun was the centre of the universe, Galileo remained briefly at Villa Medici before returning to Florence and remaining more or less under house arrest – and the protection and patronage of the Medici – for the rest of his life.

north of Rome centro storico and near the Spanish Steps and Piazza del Popolo. Given its dominant location overlooking the heart of Rome, it's no surprise that site had long been inhabited – the first home and gardens on the site are thought to date to 60 BCE. It's unclear what became of the space between the fall of the Roman Empire and the acquisition of the property by influential Cardinal Giovanni Ricci in the mid-sixteenth century. Ricci began the construction of a villa and extensive gardens, but his project was never realised.

After Ricci's death, the property was purchased in 1576 by the Grand Duke of Tuscany Ferdinando I de' Medici, son of Cosimo I de' Medici, a direct descendant of the family line that started the Medici Bank Florence, the original source of the family's historical levels of wealth. And even if later Medici no longer had Papal ambitions, they still wielded considerable influence in banking, with Ferdinando I proving his abilities both

Rear façade of
Villa Medici.
Jean-Pierre Dalbéra/CC2.0

as a financier and as a political figure, particularly in Tuscany. In Rome, the family required a prominent foothold, and Villa Medici, as the property became known, provided this.

Ferdinando I commissioned two prominent Florentines: architect Bartolomeo Ammannati to expand the building and painter Jacopo Zucchi, a painter in the style now known as Mannerism, to adorn its exterior and interior walls of his newly acquired villa in Rome.

The front façade of Villa Medici gives some clues to the break from Renaissance aesthetic that would take place behind the villa walls. Instead of rows of uniform windows on every level, the four storeys of Villa Medici alternate between rectangular and nearly squared-off, and a monumental entrance door features oversized, Doric pillars.

The rejection of the Renaissance rules are in full evidence on the rear, or north-east, façade, to the point that entering through the front façade and exiting through the rear feels like stepping into one building and stepping out of another. Ornate bas-relief sculptures are inset between windows, and empty, low-relief arched and circular niches are set at regular intervals and serve a strictly decorative purpose. Gone is the solidity and uniformity of the exterior

Detail of the rear façade of Villa Medici.
Jean-Pierre Dalbéra/CC2.0

of the Palazzo Farnese, replaced with a gloriously busy pattern of arches, insets, garlands and carved portraits. Broken pediments – where the normally curved or triangular window pediment features a gap, or a break and which would become a hallmark of the Baroque – make an early appearance here. Mannerist architecture is characterised by these architectonic details, which play with space and depth in purely aesthetic ways. While the front façade may have emphasised the stately, noble nature of the Medici dukes, the rear façade demonstrated their interest in celebrating beauty and aesthetics – a sort of 'art for art's sake' ethos centuries before that term would be used by nineteenth-century aesthetes.

Inside Villa Medici, the lines between art and architecture blur. Much of the villa's interior went through redesigns and refurbishments over time, but on a broad scope, the rooms follow the principles of Mannerist design: heavy artifice, bright colours, distortion of space and perspective, and exaggerated representations of people and things. Much like the contorted, elongated, and emotionally charged depictions of

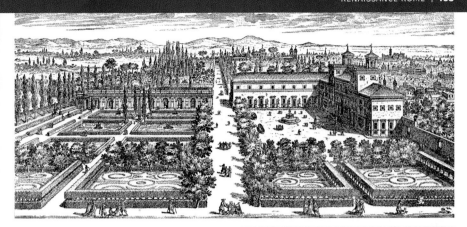

17th-century etching of the Villa Medici and gardens by Giovanni Battista Falda.

humans seen in Mannerist paintings, the architecture of the period also plays with preconceived concepts of shape and space.

By 1587, Ferdinando I de' Medici had returned to his duties in Florence, and many artistic works in the villa remained unfinished. Villa Medici was passed down to Medici males until the 1737 death of Grand Duke of Tuscany Gian Gastone de' Medici, the last of the Medici line. By that point, the Medici power had waned in Rome, and they had little reason to visit the villa. As Gian Gastone de' Medici was the last male heir, the palace and grounds went through ownership by several other wealthy Roman families, eventually ending up in possession of Napoleon Bonaparte after he annexed the region during his conquests of the eighteenth century. In 1803, Bonaparte made Villa Medici the home of the French Academy in Rome.

Salon ceiling at Villa Medici by Mannerist painter Jacopo Zucchi. sailko/CC3.0

ⓘ

HOW TO SEE IT: The interior and extensive formal gardens of Villa Medici are open to visitors Tuesday to Sunday from 9.30 am to 5.30 pm. To reach the villa, climb the Spanish Steps to via della Trinità dei Monti, then turn left and walk about two minutes to the villa entrance. Admission is currently €12 per person. Guided tours are available several times a day; check the website for current information. **https://www. villamedici.it/en/about/visits/**

BIRTHPLACE OF THE BAROQUE

Piazza Barberini, Sant'Ivo alla Sapienza & St Peter's Basilica

No architectural and artistic period is more closely associated with Rome than the Baroque. While the style manifested in regional variations throughout Europe in the 1600s, it was born in Rome and permeates the architectural aesthetic here as in perhaps no other city in the world.

In the most fundamental terms, Baroque architecture in Rome is characterised by its often massive proportions, theatrical use of light and dark, and extreme use of colour, sculptural elements and trompe-l'oeil to create an exaggerated, dramatic experience. The rationality of the Renaissance, already starting to fade in importance with the rise of Mannerism in the second-half of the sixteenth century, was fully abandoned – and with wild abandon – by the turn of the 1600s.

That the Baroque found its creative origins in Rome, the cradle of Catholicism, was no coincidence. The church had been successful in minimising the Reformation's influence within the Italian peninsula, but for the first time in more than a millennium,

it felt the pressure of competition for the hearts of the faithful. While nascent Protestant sects espoused virtue and closeness to God through humility and good works, the Catholic church turned to what it knew – the construction and adornment of both public spaces and houses of worship that were intended to overwhelm, intimidate, and demonstrate the power, wealth and righteousness of the church and the papacy.

Decades after the devastating 1527 Sack of Rome, its effects were still evident. While grand building projects were still underway well into the 1500s, Rome was far from being a model Renaissance city – for everyday Romans it was dirty, malodorous, disease-ridden, and dangerous after dark. Pope Sixtus V, though seated for only five years until his death in 1590, undertook an ambitious urban transformation of the city. Old aqueducts were restored, new ones were constructed, and periphery marshes were drained to improve the flow of the Tiber. Large swaths of Rome's confused warren of Medieval streets were razed, replaced with wide, straight thoroughfares punctuated by grand piazzas, usually adjacent to the city's most important pilgrimage destinations. Even today, the streets that fan out diagonally from the Piazza del Popolo, San Giovanni in Laterano, St Peter's and Santa Maria Maggiore all follow the urban design of this period.

Later Popes, especially Urban VIII, Innocent X and Alexander VII, who ruled consecutively from 1623 to 1667, continued Sixtus V's efforts to reclaim the city from years of degradation and further raise its visual appeal to arriving pilgrims. Their mission – or more specifically the mission with which they charged their chief architects and artists – was to create a city filled with dazzling, art-filled churches and magnificent piazzas. The desired effect was for viewers to be awestruck, both by the unmatched beauty of the spaces and the unrivalled wealth and potency of the church.

The forty-four years of combined rule of these three Popes marked the peak period of the Roman Baroque, established Rome as the most important artistic centre in Europe, and assured that works of artist-architects Gian Lorenzo Bernini and Francesco Borromini would define the aesthetic identity of the Eternal City.

Palazzo Barberini

A century before the Barberini clan raised their grand palace at this location on the north-west side of Rome's Quirinal Hill, the property belonged to the Sforza family, who once controlled Milan and had ties to the Holy Roman Empire. As the Sforza fortunes faded in the sixteenth century, the family began unloading assets, including their compound on Quirinal Hill. The Florence-born Barberini were rivals of the Medici, who controlled Florence. Several family members fled Florence for Rome, where their ascension to power reached its peak with the 1623 election of Maffeo Barberini to the Papal throne. He ruled as Urban VIII, and purchased the Sforza property in 1625.

An 18th-C engraving of Palazzo Barberini, by Giovanni Piranesi.

In the epitome of papal nepotism, Urban VIII installed several family members into the church, including three relatives appointed cardinals, a brother named as a duke in Rome, and a nephew appointed Prince of Palestrina, a territory just east of Rome. When Pope Urban VIII purchased the site, the property housed a small home built by the Sforza family. This building later became part of an enormous new palace, which Urban VIII ordered built as a means of cementing – literally and figuratively – the Barberini status in Rome.

Carlo Maderno began the design in 1627, in partnership with his nephew and protégé Francesco Borromini. Upon Maderno's death in 1629, Gian Lorenzo Bernini, the favoured artist of the Barberini, was appointed chief architect. At that point Bernini was still known primarily as a sculptor, and that he was chosen over Borromini would doubtlessly have been an insult and embarrassment to the older architect and assistant to Maderno. Borromini continued to work on the project after Bernini's appointment and by some accounts, the two architects worked collaboratively during some phases of construction. Each left their distinct handprints on a palace, though it was Bernini who saw the project through to its completion in 1633.

West façade of Palazzo Barberini, with top floor windows by Borromini. Jean-Pierre Dalbéra/CC2.0

Gardens of Palazzo Barberini. Jean-Pierre Dalbéra/CC2.0

Like the Barberini rivals the Farnese (see sidebar, below) had done at Palazzo Farnese nearly a century earlier, Urban VIII commissioned Palazzo Barberini to be opulent and impressive. Architects Maderno, Borromini and – perhaps to a greater extent – Bernini understood their dual tasks of creating something that was both awe-inspiring to the public and obsequious of a difficult, powerful patron-client. At the same time, they sought to create a design that was of its time, that reflected the aesthetic liberty of the post-Renaissance era and that would confirm Rome's status as the epicentre of a new architectural style.

Urban VIII required that his new palazzo house in princely comfort two of his cardinal nephews and their families. This living arrangement alone necessitated a break from traditional palazzo design, in that the nephews each required their own equally resplendent quarters. The solution was to divide the palace into two immense, private wings connected by a three-storey façade and a ground-floor loggia. The innovation of Maderno's original design is that it breaks from the traditional blocky, square plan of a palace with three or four sides that are more or less equal in size and appearance, surrounding a central courtyard. Instead Maderno designed an open, H-shaped structure that was more

Borromini-designed staircase at Palazzo Barberini.
Sailko/CC3.0

in keeping with the style of a country villa than an urban palace.

It's also believed that the slope of the Quirinal Hill necessitated a wider, more spread-out design, rather than the large, deep rectangular shape of similar noble palaces. The result was remarkable for its era and genre, with the airy ground-floor loggia connecting to an immense formal garden, and the two wings functioning almost as separate households.

Given the overlap in architects – Maderno and Borromini, then Bernini and Borromini – it's not possible to attribute all the design elements to just one designer or design phase. It's generally understood that the footprint is attributable to Maderno, and that Bernini and Borromini largely adhered to his design, while presumably adding more of the elements that we now associate with Baroque style – including exterior elements like the arched window lintels, carved garlands and greenery, and first-floor pilasters.

That said, there are specific elements of Palazzo Barberini for which each architect is remembered. To Borromini, scholars credit the row of windows on the top floor of the west entrance. Here, the architect utilised false perspective – the windows are set back from the plane of the façade, surrounded by a frame that angles inward and topped by a shallow arch that makes it wider at the top than at the sides, giving the appearance of being set deeper back than they really are. This would become an exceedingly Baroque tradition – an architectural trompe l'oeil to create drama and depth for an imposing and intense first impression.

Defining each wing is a monumental staircase. In the southern wing is one of Borromini's most magnificent works – a three-storey helicoidal, or oval-shaped, staircase, supported by pairs of Tuscan, or simplified Doric order, columns. The staircase undulates upwards like a graceful, fluid stone wave, towards a rooftop window through which light pours downwards.

Bernini-designed staircase at Palazzo Barberini.
Sailko/CC3.0

In the opposite wing, and Bernini's staircase is the angular response to Borromini's curved version, and seems to suggest that the two architects were in a collaborative phase when both staircases were completed. Bernini's stairs also span three levels, and are defined by pairs of Tuscan/Doric columns that serve as the staircase's outer supports, and false windows along the staircase's inner silo add depth and create shadows in the light from the open-air skylight above. On both sets of stairs, the signature Barberini bees are carved into the column and pilaster capitals.

Bernini is also credited with the central two-storey entrance hall, the ceiling of which was frescoed by Pietro da Cortona. The latter's vastly unsubtle Allegory of Divine Providence and Barberini Power is the stunning focal point of the palazzo, an overwhelmingly busy and dizzying composition of trompe l'oeil painted architectonic elements, mythological and liturgical figures. The painted rectangular frame of the composition is broken by figures within and outside of the central panel, as if their energy can't be contained by the faux-stone confines. As the title suggests, the fresco depicts allegorical figures presenting the Papal keys and vestments to a swarm of Barberini bees, signalling the divine destiny by which Maffeo Barberini ascended to the papal throne. Cortona's Allegory was one of the last major works to be completed at the palace, and would become a

Right: **Allegory of Divine Providence and Barberini Power** *by Pietro da Cortona.* Livioandronico2013/CC4.0

veritable prototype for the riotous Baroque frescoes that would follow in the seventeenth century, particularly in Roman churches and basilicas.

Descendants of the Barberini lived in the palazzo until the mid-1950s, when it became the seat of the National Gallery of Antique Art. The collection includes works from the eleventh through the eighteenth centuries, including outstanding masterworks from Raphael and Caravaggio. Its stunning interiors are as much the draw as the art collection, as visitors access the two exquisite staircases, Cortona's frescoed ceiling, and formal gardens that lie hidden behind the palace's perimeter walls. On the extensive grounds are the remains of a Mithraeum thought to date to the second century.

HOW TO SEE IT: The National Gallery of Antique Art at Palazzo Barberini is located at Via delle Quattro Fontane 13, about a 15–20 minute walk from Termini Station. It is also adjacent to the Barberini metro stop and served by several bus routes. Current hours are Tuesday to Sunday from 8.30 am to 7 pm. Admission is €12, and includes access to the Galleria Corsini, which is also a branch of the National Gallery of Antique Art. The combined ticket is valid for ten days. For more information, visit **www.barberinicorsini.org/en**.

A most notorious Pope

As a patron of the arts, Pope Urban VIII was responsible for commissioning some of the most exceptional artistic endeavours in Rome, and championing the work of Gian Lorenzo Bernini. But little else complimentary can be said about the legacy of Maffeo Barberini, whose years on the papal throne were defined by nepotism, ego, and aggression for the sake of personal gain. He installed no less than five family members into high-ranking positions within the church immediately upon his ascension to the throne and appointed both his brother Carlo and nephew Taddeo as gonfalonier of the church, which meant they led the papal armies. He started several wars with neighbouring regions, over what were essentially insults to his family. Even amid centuries of papal excesses, Urban VIII ranks among the most notorious and excessive.

Interestingly, Urban VIII was a friend and patron to Galileo Galilei, and supported his work despite the fact that much of it was perceived to challenge church doctrine. Urban VIII encouraged the scientist's research into heliocentrism

Portrait of Urban VIII by Pietro da Cortona, ca.1624-1627.

– the theory that the earth revolved around the sun – until the publication of Galileo's Dialogue Concerning the Two Chief Systems of the World in 1632. Pope Urban VIII felt as though he had been portrayed in a way that was embarrassing to the church and, more importantly, to him personally, and he ordered Galileo to defend and recant his viewpoints. Famously, Galileo stuck to his convictions and was sentenced to house arrest until his death in 1642.

Pope Urban VIII's reign ended upon his death in 1644, by which point he was already exceedingly unpopular. His wars and excesses left Rome nearly bankrupt, and after his death much of his family had to flee Rome. Giovanni Battista Pamphilj – long Urban VIII's biggest rival in the cardinalate – was elected Pope and took the name Innocent X, a not-so-subtle dig at his predecessor. Pope Urban VIII's reputation for greed, warmongering, and nepotism may explain why no Pope since then has assumed the name 'Urban'.

Sant'Ivo alla Sapienza

Among Rome's leading Baroque architects, Francesco Borromini is considered to have possessed a keener sense of the physical structure of architecture, beyond its aesthetic properties. He trained as a young man in building and stonemasonry, the tenets of which he carried into his work as an architect. Bernini, his sometime colleague and more frequently, chief rival, was heralded for his celebration of the human form as realised architectonically. Borromini, instead, is remembered for his use of geometry as the basis for his designs, and for his willingness to break the rectilinear properties of the wall in order to challenge the traditional conventions of space. His complex mix of geometry, spatial relationships and the use of light as an architectural element are elegantly, surprisingly presented at the church of Sant'Ivo alla Sapienza.

When, in 1642 he was commissioned to create a new chapel for the palace of La Sapienza, the name of the University of Rome, Borromini was presented with a set of limitations. The exterior of the Palazzo alla Sapienza was (and remains) a blocky, stoic building with a front, street-side section and a right and left wing. These three sides wrap around an open courtyard designed a half-century earlier by Giacomo della Porta and in the Mannerist style. The three-level courtyard has two stories of open arcades delineated by arches, while

A 1665 engraving of Sant'Ivo alla Sapienza by G. B. Falda.

the façade of the third storey features S-curved, swan-neck style pediments, above which a row of circular insets contain sculpted bees – the symbol for the Barberini family, who were both the patrons of La Sapienza and the family of Pope Urban VIII.

Borromini's task was to work within the confines of the existing courtyard, to add at its open end a chapel dedicated to Sant'Ivo, the patron saint of lawyers. His solution was absolutely novel – a star-shaped building with a curved façade that serves to continue, rather than cut off, the harmonious arch patterns of della Porta's courtyard.

Borromini's design was revolutionary in that it 'broke the wall' – instead of closing the courtyard with the predictable straight-walled façade of the new church, he created a graceful concave form, which carries the viewer's eye from the courtyard's rows of arches to the entrance of the church. It's been likened that the wings of the palazzo are the arms of the church, reaching out to envelop all those who approach, and that the open space of the courtyard itself becomes an element in the architecture of the church.

Borromini continued the pattern of arches on the first two levels of the façade, as well as the Doric pilasters of the first level and the Ionic pilasters of the second. On top of, and behind the concave façade, Borromini juxtaposed the convexly curved, hexagonal drum

The cupola of Sant'Ivo alla Sapienza.
Stefano80/CC3.0

of the dome, whose plump sections are delineated by Corinthian pilasters. Sitting on top of the dome is a lantern, capped with a corkscrew-shaped spire that finishes in a crown topped by a cross – emblematic of the search for wisdom in service of Christ and the church.

The exterior of Sant'Ivo alla Sapienza is recognised for its architectural innovations, but its interior is no less important in demonstrating Borromini's use of geometry. He chose a rounded,

The dome of Sant'Ivo alla Sapienza. Archidas/CC 4.0

six-point star shape, which at the time represented the Star of Solomon, a symbol of wisdom. (It wasn't until the nineteenth century that the Star of Solomon, also known as the Star of David, became more exclusively a symbol of Judaism.) When one is standing in the centre of the rotunda, the geometric forms of two overlaid triangles are revealed, with one triangle's points cut off in concave forms and the others in widely arcing circles. A radiating star pattern emanates from the centre-point of the black and white floor tile, which was

Borromini's design for the dome of Sant'Ivo.

also Borromini's design.

The concave and convex juxtaposition continues upwards, in the intricate, delicate dome, where light floods in through six windows and the

Duelling Papal Insignias

Borromini worked on Sant'Ivo from 1632 and 1667, and served three Popes in the process. They too, left their marks on the church, in the form of their family insignias. Pope Urban VIII was a Barberini, and his family symbol of the bee features prominently in the courtyard – though subsequent Popes apparently removed several conspicuous bee carvings inside the church. Succeeding Urban VIII, Pope Innocent was a Pamphilj. His family symbol, the dove with an olive branch and the fleur de lys, appears on a medallion on the drum, overlooking the courtyard, on the lantern and at points inside the rotunda. Pope Alexander VII, of the Chigi family, left the most obtrusive and inelegant of insignias – his family symbol of six mountains under an eight-point star, which appears on three sections of the dome. Large, three-dimensional versions of the Chigi symbol cap each end of the façade, and the eight-point star motif is repeated throughout the interior and exterior.

windows of the lantern, and sets the white stucco aglow.

Borromini's work at Sant'Ivo was first greeted with admiration, which less than a century later turned to disdain. The rationality and order of neoclassicism meant that the complicated patterns and decorative nature of Borromini's work was scoffed at, and the church fell out of fashion as an architectural monument. Sant'Ivo's was deconsecrated in the early twentieth century, and was only re-consecrated after the university moved out of Palazzo alla Sapienza and into a new campus near present-day Termini station. The palazzo became the headquarters of the state archives, and remains so today. Only after the Second World War was Sant'Ivo's again recognised as an important architectural monument.

HOW TO SEE IT: The entrance to Sant'Ivo della Sapienza is from the della Porta courtyard and within the Palazzo alla Sapienza, now the Archivio di Stato di Roma, or State Archives. Though you should be able to step into the courtyard and see Borromini's façade any time during regular business hours, the church itself is only open on Sunday mornings from 10 am to 12 pm. It's closed all month during July and August. Because it is a popular destination for architecture aficionados, it's best to arrive a little before 10 am and wait for the doors to open. The entrance is at Corso del Rinascimento 40, the main thoroughfare just east of Piazza Navona. Note that Mass is observed at 11 am on Sundays, during which time it is disrespectful to take photographs or walk around inside the church. More information (in Italian only) is available at **http://www.sivoallasapienza.eu/**.

Bernini & St Peter's Basilica

The history of St Peter's Basilica is long, the building is immense, and its phases of design, construction and renovation could – and do – fill volumes. The hands of countless artists, architects, stonemasons, and craftspeople have left their mark on St Peter's. Some of them are known to us – Giotto, Canova, Bramante, Raphael and others – while still untold more laboured in anonymity or have had their names lost to time. Michelangelo adapted the designs of his predecessors to create much of the present-day interior architecture of St Peter's including its soaring dome, but he did not live to see his project realised. This was not the case for Gian Lorenzo Bernini,

who worked for more than fifty years on the basilica, and lived to see realised his designs for its colonnaded piazza, magnificent baldachin structure over the tomb of St Peter, and numerous other Papal tombs and embellishments within. It is Bernini more than any other who left the Baroque stamp on St Peter's and who is most responsible – and remembered – for the basilica's current appearance.

By the time he moved with his family from Naples to Rome in 1606, then 8-year-old Gian Lorenzo Bernini was already considered an artistic child prodigy. He soon found a patron in Cardinal Scipione Borghese, nephew to Pope Paul V. Borghese commissioned several works of art, which in the space of just a few years established Bernini, still in his twenties, as the master sculptor of his time. His masterpieces, including Apollo and Daphne and David, both viewable in the Galleria Borghese, demonstrated, in solid white marble, a sense of emotion, movement and drama that had few equals in the history of Western art. When depicting mythological subject matter, he captured a specific dramatic moment – for example, his David bites his lower lip as his body twists in motion, the exact moment before he hurls a stone at the giant Goliath. By comparison, Michelangelo's David is concentrated, stoic and motionless, while Bernini's is all emotion, action and dramatic tension. In his work at St Peter's, he imparted this same sense of emotion, and represented the curvature and movement of the human body in architectural forms.

Bernini was already the favoured artist and architect of the Barberini family when Maffeo Barberini was elected to the Papal throne in 1623. In 1629, after the death of Carlo Maderno, Bernini – just 31 years old – was appointed chief architect of St Peter's and charged with continuing a restoration and expansion of the basilica that had been ongoing for more than a century. He inherited works in progress and the plans of preceding architects for most of the more significant components of the basilica.

The baldachin of St Peter's Basilica. Jorge Royan. CC3.0

Detail of the baldachin of St Peter's Basilica.
Herb Neufeld/CC2.0

And although he worked in collaboration with Francesco Borromini (before their rivalry intensified), it is Bernini alone whose name is associated with the monumental Baldacchino di San Pietro, or St Peter's Baldachin.

The 95-ft-tall baldachin is the bronze canopy which forms the focal point and ultimate destination within the basilica. The concept of the baldachin refers to Catholic convention of a cloth canopy over sacred spots, or as a protective awning carried over the Pope. The baldachin of St Peter's sits under Michelangelo's soaring dome and over the tomb of St Peter, the most important and sacred area of the basilica. Bernini's baldachin is as much sculptural as it is architectural, and is regarded as the first of his works to fully meld these two disciplines and demonstrate his mastery of both.

The baldachin's dominant feature are the four spiralling, or helical, columns that hold up the massive canopy. These 66-ft-tall bronze columns intentionally mimic the spiral columns which had previously stood near the tomb, and which were allegedly pillaged from the Hebrew Temple of Solomon in Jerusalem and brought to Rome by Constantine. These eight older, marble columns now form decorative elements in the four piers – also designed by Bernini – that support the dome. Apart from the four marble plinths on which the helical

Labour Pains?

The giant columns of the baldachin of St Peter rest on four, four-sided marble plinths as intricately decorated as the rest of the monument. Two sides of each plinth are set with shields of the Barberini family coat of arms, which includes three of the familiar bees. At the top of each of the eight shields is a woman's face, and each face is different. Starting from the plinth on the front left-hand side (facing the entrance), and viewed clockwise, the woman's expression changes from calm and composed to dishevelled and screaming – with the last face replaced by the face of a winged baby, or putto. The sequence represents the stages of childbirth, but Bernini's motives for the cycle remain unresolved. A nobler theory maintains that Bernini intended to represent the labours and rewards of the papacy. Another, more tantalising claim is that Bernini hid the symbolic sequence in the baldachin as revenge against Alexander VII, who refused to recognise an illegitimate child born to his nephew, Cardinal Taddeo Barberini, and the sister of one of Bernini's assistants.

columns rest, the entire structure is composed of intricate cast bronze. The scalloped roof of the baldachin was designed to look like the cloth of the traditional papal canopy, and is decorated with the Barberini bees, as well as symbols of the radiant sun, intended to represent both the Holy Spirit and Pope Urban VIII's family. Cherubs hold the papal keys and tiara over the Barberini insignias, while from each corner of the roof, four larger-than-life-sized angels look down on worshippers below.

Visible beyond the baldachin at the far end of the basilica, Bernini's Cathedra Petri is a massive chair built to house the relic of the throne of St Peter, which most likely dates to centuries later than the time of Peter the Apostle. Bernini completed the work, made entirely of bronze, in the 1660s, when he had already been working at St Peter's for nearly four decades. The throne is surrounded by sculptures of the four doctors of the church and rises, seemingly weightlessly, on a billow of clouds, from which a riot of angels and cherubs emerge. In the centrepiece of the vignette, above the throne, a stained-glass window of the dove of peace glows with white and golden light.

To the left of the throne and baldachin, the Monument to Pope Alexander VII was the last work of the great sculptor and architect, completed in 1678 when Bernini was 80 years old. Alexander VII, who was Pope from 1655

The Cathedra Petri. Dnalor/CC3.0

The tomb monument to Pope Alexander VII.
Jean-Pol GRANDMONT/CC3.0

to 1667, had commissioned Bernini to design his grandiose tomb monument well before his death. Work did not begin on the tomb until several years after the Pope's death, but Bernini achieved Alexander VII's desire to leave an enduring papal monument. And, perhaps because an aging Bernini was contemplating his own mortality – he died in 1680, just two years after the tomb was finished – the funerary

monument is among his most haunting. An oversized statue of the Pope, shown kneeling in prayer, commands the top of the monument. Allegorical figures of Truth, Justice, Charity and Prudence surround the Pope. They rest on top of a heavy marble drapery, from under which emerges the figure of Death, depicted as a bronze, winged skeleton, gesturing towards Alexander VII with an hourglass in his hand – a momento mori, or reminder that Death comes for everyone, regardless of their status in life. The eerie figure, its face and head obscured by the drapery, writhes and floats while the other figures seem anchored in time and space – and serves as a sharp, ominous contrast to their tranquillity and piety.

Bernini's most readily visible contribution to St Peter's is the huge piazza in front of the basilica, which Alexander VII commissioned him to finish in 1656. The architect conceived the vast open space, ringed by two curved colonnades, or columned walkways, as symbolising the welcoming arms of the basilica and the Catholic church itself.

But the space Bernini inherited for the piazza had limitations around which he had to adjust his design, including the Maderno-designed façade, completed in 1612, and an enormous obelisk in the centre of the piazza. Brought from Egypt by Caligula, the obelisk had been erected in the Circus of Nero in 37 CE, and is said to have 'stood witness' to the crucifixion of

Piazza San Pietro as seen from the dome of the basilica. valyag/CC3.0

Aerial view of St Peter's in 1922, before the creation of Via della Conciliazione.

Peter at that site. The obelisk's symbolic, spiritual and historical importance meant that Bernini had to build his piazza around it. To the right of the obelisk, a fountain designed by Maderno was already in place.

Bernini designed a matching fountain to be set to the left of the obelisk, but was still faced with the conundrum of what form the piazza should take.

A rectangular piazza, with the obelisk at its centre, would have required the demolition of several nearby Papal buildings, and its vast size would have minimised the importance of Maderno's façade. His innovative solution was to divide the piazza into two parts – the colonnaded oval that embraces visitors, and the trapezoidal shaped portion closest to the basilica, that widens at the end closest to the façade. This makes the façade look closer and taller than it actually is, and minimises the width of the façade, which had long been a criticism of the Maderno design.

For more than 250 years after its completion, pilgrims and visitors made their way to St Peter's Basilica via an area of densely set residential houses and narrow streets. When they emerged from these tight, dark confines onto the open vastness of Piazza San Pietro and its sweeping colonnades, they must have felt as though they were arriving in Paradise itself. This effect, called the 'Baroque Surprise' of St Peter's, lasted until 1936, when Mussolini ordered the demolition of the Medieval and Renaissance neighbourhood outside St Peter's. In its place now is the long, wide promenade of Via della Conciliazione, which, while continuing the monumental and theatrical approach to St Peter's, destroyed forever an essential part of the experience of arriving at the basilica.

Still, Bernini's piazza, which was largely completed by 1667, fully represents the Baroque concept of breaking the frame – of challenging the space between subject and viewer and of imbuing a sense of unrestrained emotion and movement. The façade of St Peter's becomes part of the set – not merely the backdrop but the focal point – of the stage that is St Peter's Square, and visitors are drawn to the basilica – enveloped by it, really – long before they reach its doors. If the Baroque aesthetic philosophy can be described as one of pulling viewers close with theatrical emotion, overwhelming scale and

artistic and architectural *trompe l'oeil*, Piazza San Pietro is the *magnum opus*, of both Bernini's long and illustrious career and the era of Roman Baroque architecture.

HOW TO SEE IT: St Peter's Basilica is open every day from 7 am to 7 pm from April to September, and to 6 pm from October to March. St Peter's Square is always open. Admission is free. Lines to enter the basilica are often very long and while they keep moving, it's not unusual to wait in line an hour or more during peak season. Plan to arrive first thing in the morning or late in the afternoon for the shortest wait times. The alternative is to book a self-guided 'skip the line' tour through Vox Mundi (**www.voxmundi.eu/**), the official tour provider for the basilica. Tours start at €23.

The basilica is 1.5 miles, or about a thirty to thirty-five minute walk from Piazza Venezia, and twenty minutes from Piazza Navona. The closest Metro stop is Ottaviano, a ten minute walk from the basilica.

All visitors to the basilica must dress modestly, which means no shorts or skirts above the knee, no sleeveless or low-cut shirts and no hats. These guidelines apply for men and women and are strictly enforced. For more information, visit **www. vaticanstate.va/content/vaticanstate/ en/informazioni-utili.html**.

A City of Fountains

While seventeenth-century Popes were engaged with building projects at Vatican City and the construction or renovation of churches all over the city, they also turned their attention to vanity projects intended to earn the loyalty and admiration of the Roman people. The development of Piazza Navona, Piazza del Popolo and the Spanish Steps (Piazza Spagna) date to this period. But the secular landmarks most associated with Roman Baroque, and most fondly appreciated to this day, are undoubtedly the monumental fountains created in the 1600s, many the work of or directly influenced by Bernini:

- Pope Innocent X commissioned Bernini to design the breath-taking Fountain of the Four Rivers as the focal point of Piazza Navona.

- Though not completed until the 1760s, when the Baroque style was falling well out of fashion, the Trevi Fountain, Rome's largest

Fountain of the Four Rivers.

Triton Fountain.

Trevi Fountain.

fountain and a veritable symbol of the Baroque, was first commissioned by Pope Urban VIII in the 1630s. Bernini, da Cortona and Mannerist architect Alessandro Galilei all competed to design it, though none lived to see it completed.

● Traffic races around the Fontana del Tritone (Triton Fountain), where a sinewy sea-god Triton rides atop a base adorned with four dolphins and the Barberini bees – the fountain was commissioned by Urban VIII for the piazza in front of Palazzo Barberini.

● The Barberini bees also buzz at the comparatively modest Fontana della Barcaccia, designed by Bernini as the grace note at the foot of the Spanish Steps.

Beyond their considerable aesthetic merits, these fountains and others throughout the city,

Fontana della Barcaccia.

brought clean water to the streets of Rome – and their construction was a sure way for shrewd Popes to curry favour with the people.

NEOCLASSICAL SOBRIETY

St John in Lateran, Palazzo Braschi & the Vittorio Emanuele monument

By the early decades of the 1700s, the Baroque style of art and architecture had evolved – or devolved, depending on one's taste – into the frenzied excessiveness of the Rococo. Once considered part of Late Baroque style but now recognised as a separate artistic period, the Rococo was characterised, in art, architecture and furniture design, by its extreme ornamentation, gilt, high relief and theatricality. Rococo palaces and churches, particularly their interiors, are overwhelming in detail and decoration. The visual 'noise' they create could be likened to a musical crescendo: the final, rousing, emotional act of a style – and a period in European history – that was coming to a close. And the abandonment of the ornamentation of the Baroque and the frivolity of the Rococo can be linked to several overlapping developments in eighteenth-century Europe

By the early decades of the 1700s, the Baroque style of art and architecture had evolved – or devolved, depending on one's taste – into the frenzied excessiveness of the Rococo. Once considered part of Late Baroque style but now recognised as a separate artistic period, the Rococo was characterised, in art, architecture and furniture design, by its extreme ornamentation, gilt, high relief and theatricality. Rococo palaces and churches, particularly their interiors, are overwhelming in detail and decoration. The visual 'noise' they create could be likened to a musical crescendo: the final, rousing, emotional act of a style – and a period in European history – that was coming to a close. And the abandonment of the ornamentation of the Baroque and the frivolity of the Rococo can be linked to several overlapping developments in

Riotous rococo: The circa 1730s Gallery of Mirrors at the Palazzo Doria Pamphilj, Rome. Sailko/CC3.0

eighteenth-century Europe.

From a European socio-political standpoint, the excesses of the Baroque and Rococo periods were emblematic of monarchies and aristocracies grossly out-of-touch with and unconcerned by the hardships of their less-fortunate subjects. The stirrings of revolution in France and the American Colonies, and the increasingly diminished governing role of the British monarchy did not have direct impact on papal or aristocratic supremacy in Italy. But the threat of a desperate, dissatisfied and possibly mutinous population did awaken Rome's ruling classes to the possibility of popular unrest and the need to exercise some restraint – or at least the appearance of restraint – in the face it presented to the public.

Intellectually, the artists, architects and philosophers of the period that would become known as the Enlightenment looked, as their Renaissance predecessors had done, to the treatises of ancient Greece and Rome as models for the study of natural sciences, political science and philosophy. The Enlightenment diverged from the Renaissance in terms of the former's increasing embracement of secularism, as religion (in its Catholic and, now, Protestant forms) exerted less and less influence on science and education. While the Renaissance celebrated the perfection of human capabilities in the service of the Christian (Catholic) God, the Enlightenment questioned the very nature of God and the state of the human condition. The intellectual and political revolutions of the Enlightenment would help foment the coming Risorgimento, the Italian unification movement of the nineteenth century.

Culturally, the Enlightenment's referral to the models of ancient Greece and Rome brought a renewed interest in these epochs across all fields of study and artistic endeavour. Archaeological excavations at Pompeii and Herculaneum, which had been rediscovered in the 1730s, enabled artists and architects to see, for the first time, what the interiors and (to a lesser extent) exteriors of Roman domestic and municipal buildings really looked like. The influence these excavations had on the cultural output of the Enlightenment/neoclassical era simply can't be overstated. While Renaissance architecture looked to the architectonic ruins of ancient Rome for the inspiration for their designs, neoclassical architects considered the ancient Greek and Roman remains as the ideal architectural model, one which there was little need to modify. Pompeii and Herculaneum completed the picture of the Roman past and in the Eternal City, their influence was strongly felt.

The Archbasilica of St John Lateran

There's been a place of worship on the site of the Archbasilica of St John Lateran, also known as San Giovanni in Laterano, or the Lateran Basilica, since the fourth century, when newly victorious Emperor Constantine gave the site to the Bishop of Rome (the Pope). In 324, it was named the Lateran Palace and the seat of the church. Even today, while St Peter's Basilica is the closest to the Pope's official residence in Vatican City, St John Lateran is the Pope's 'mother church', and spiritually the most important basilica – and the only one with the title 'archbasilica' – in the Catholic faith. The complex's timeline, both historically and architecturally, is long and tumultuous, but the present façade dates to 1735 and aptly represents the transition from the Rococo to neoclassical style of architecture.

The Lateran Basilica and its adjacent papal residence, the Lateran Palace, takes its name from any of several individuals from the family Sextius

The façade of San Giovanni in Laterano ca 1765, etching by Giovanni Vasi.

Lateranus, who were among the first plebeians (plebs), or commoners, to achieve important ranks in Republican Rome. The family was influential through the end of the Republic and into the first centuries of the Roman Empire, and its members served several emperors. The last member of the Laterani line, Titus Sextius Magius Lateranus, was known to have served Emperor Septimus Severus at the end of the second century CE. Severus built a military fort adjacent to Titus Lateranus' palace – hence the Lateran Palace – on the Caelian Hill, about 2 km east-south-east of the Colosseum.

After Constantine defeated Maxentius at the Battle of the Milvian Bridge in 312, he ordered the fort destroyed and took possession of the Lateran Palace, which by then belonged to his second wife, Fausta, who was also the sister of Maxentius. The transfer of the palace to the papacy appears to have occurred shortly after 312, with Pope Sylvester I (seated 314–34) the first Bishop of Rome to reside in the Lateran Palace. The palace, which would have had a basilica area for Lateranus to receive visitors and conduct business, was expanded under Sylvester and became the first Cathedral of Rome. The first basilica, of which we know very little design-wise, was destroyed by an earthquake in 897. It was rebuilt soon after, according to a footprint that very likely followed the original floorplan and the familiar basilica style of a central nave and two aisles.

The Lateran Archbasilica and palace

A Grateful Constantine

The history of the earliest decades of the Catholic church are murky at best, but Constantine is known to have been very generous to the church when Sylvester I was Pope, including his gifting of the Lateran Palace. A legend, probably developed in the sixth century, records that Pope Sylvester I cured Constantine of leprosy and to show his generosity, Constantine granted Sylvester and the church not just the Lateran Palace but supremacy over all of Rome. Shortly after, Constantine left Rome for Constantinople and essentially left Sylvester and successive Popes in charge. Evidence of the 'Donation of Constantine', as the transfer of power came to be known, was used to establish the church's claim to lands once controlled by the Roman Empire. It was widely accepted as a forgery by the 1400s.

was the home of every Pope and the seat of the church until 1309 when the papacy moved to Avignon, France. By the time the papacy returned to Rome in 1376, the complex had been severely damaged by two fires and was deemed uninhabitable. After the papal home transferred to St Peter's, the Lateran complex lay in disrepair for two centuries, until Pope Sixtus V ordered a concerted rebuilding. Its interior was redesigned by Francesco Borromini, who was commissioned by Pope Innocent X (seated 1644–55). Created during the height of the Roman Baroque, the massive nave bears all the hallmarks of the era and of Borromini's style, with its geometric complexity, play of light and dark colours and extensive use of high relief to create a chiaroscuro effect.

The exterior of the archbasilica was commissioned by Pope Clement XII (seated 1730–40), and is remarkable for its departure from traditional basilica design and the then-norms of the Late Baroque/Rococo. The architect, Alessandro Galilei, was known for his 'anti-Baroque' style and adherence to classical design. His work on the façade, executed in 1735, was immediately criticised as being fit for a palace but not a basilica – and the starkly different design must have indeed been shocking at the time. In place of a typically steeply gabled roof of traditional models, Galilei created a façade that resembled an ancient temple, with central, two-storey tall pediment supported by massive

The Borromini-designed interior of San Giovanni in Laterano. tango7174/CC4.0

San Giovanni in Laterano, with the Lateran Palace to the right.
Berthold Werner/Public domain

Corinthian pilasters. To each side of the main doorway are two square-roofed entries to the narthex, or open, covered porch. On the second level, five arches open to a loggia, where a series of shallow, arched niches give the illusion of receding space.

Galilei's façade contradicts traditional basilica style in that its rectangular form, broken only by the pediment and small central gable, nearly masks the presence of the wide interior nave and four side aisles. A balustrade, or low railing, runs along the roof of the structure, over which stands a statue of Christ flanked by ten saints, including St John the Baptist and St John the Evangelist, the two patrons of the archbasilica. The dramatic and powerful figures stand in exaggerated contrapposto, or counterpoised stance, carved robes rippling in movement and most gesturing in the air with one hand. While the statues echo the overstated, emotional style of the Late Baroque, the massive columns and the almost

HOW TO SEE IT: After admiring the Galilei's façade of the Archbasilica of St John Lateran (San Giovanni in Laterano), take time to explore the interiors of the vast complex, which include a sacristy, a cloister, a museum filled with papal treasures, traces of the Roman-era buildings and, of course, Borromini's spectacular Baroque nave and aisles. The archbasilica is open daily from 7.30 am to 6 pm. The museum of the archbasilica is open daily from 10 am to 5.30 pm. To reach the complex, you can take the Metro to San Giovanni station and walk about three minutes to Piazza San Giovanni in Laterano. From the Colosseum, the archbasilica is a fifteen to twenty minute walk. From central Rome, buses 51, 81, 85 or 87 are the most convenient. The archbasilica website is in Italian only, but you can check for the latest hours: **http://www.vatican.va/various/basiliche/san_giovanni/index_it.htm.**

1775 painting of Pius VI by Pompeo Batoni, National Gallery of Ireland.

impersonal feel evoked by the façade are a clear precursor to the relative eclecticism of neoclassical architecture.

Palazzo Braschi

Occupying an entire city block in densely built-up area and fronting a small piazza that doubles as a taxi stand, Palazzo Braschi looks like many of the other stately, neoclassical buildings in the surrounding neighbourhood between Campo de'Fiori and Piazza Navona,

with their neat rows of curved- and segmental-pediment windows looking down on tourists and traffic milling below. But the history of the palazzo marks a turning point in the history of Italy and Rome, and recalls the seeds of revolution, the curtailment of Papal power, the formation of the Italian state and the rise of fascism.

When Duke Luigi Braschi Onesti purchased the Renaissance-era Orsini Palace in 1790, he did so with economic support from his uncle, Giovanni Angelo Braschi, who since 1775 had reigned as Pope Pius VI. Luigi's title of Duke of Nemi, a city south-east of Rome,

Façade of Palazzo Braschi from Piazza di San Pantaleo. Achille83/Public domain

had been granted to him by Pius VI, as had a number of other titles and gifts that allowed the Papal nephew to accumulate wealth and power. The Pope approved the razing of Palazzo Orsini and, in the spirit of the Barberini and Farnese popes before him, financed the construction of a grand new family palazzo that would affirm the Braschi family status in the Eternal City.

The French Revolution had commenced in 1789, and Pius VI presumably did not anticipate the profound ripple effect it would have in the Italian peninsula. The Revolution was hostile to the papacy well before 1793, when Pius VI declared Louis XVI, the executed King of France, a martyr. Pius had long opposed the Revolution, which took control of Church assets in France. Papal troops fought against French Republican troops, who were under the command of Napoleon Bonaparte. In 1796 Napoleon's army invaded the Italian peninsula and quickly bested the papal armies. By 1798 they entered Rome and declared it the Roman Republic. When Pius VI refused to cede power, he was arrested and eventually held in Valence in southern France, where he died, still imprisoned, in 1799.

The turn of events marked the effective end of papal nepotism and more significantly, the decline of the power of the papacy. Prompted by the Revolution and the French occupation, Italy's gradual move towards a republican form of government meant that subsequent Popes would never again wield the political authority and influence that had defined centuries of history in Rome and the rest of Europe.

In the midst of all this, construction of Palazzo Braschi moved in fits and starts. Work was suspended in 1798, when the French took control of the palazzo and other properties associated

Mussolini was here

The neoclassical structures discussed in this chapter all served as the backdrop for key moments or periods of Mussolini's rule during the fascist era. The 1929 Lateran Accords, which ended decades of bitter hostility between the Catholic church and the Kingdom of Italy, were named for the Lateran Palace, where they were signed by Mussolini and a representative of Pope Pius XI. The accords created the independent state of Vatican City, giving the church the sovereignty that it had sought for years, and helping Mussolini assuage Italy's Catholic population.

Palazzo Braschi was the Fascist Party from 1922 until Mussolini's arrest in 1943. During the 1934 election campaign, Italians were asked to vote 'si' or 'no' on a slate of 400 fascist party officials nominated to the

Palazzo Braschi during the 1934 election campaign.

Chamber of Deputies – the equivalent of a parliament. All other political parties had been outlawed since 1926 and a yes vote was never in doubt. Nevertheless, a giant sculpture of Mussolini was hung on the façade of Palazzo

with the papacy. While it's not entirely clear what stage the palace had reached before work stopped in this tumultuous period, its footprint was probably close to that of the present day – and the building was at least finished enough to be occupied by French officials.

The palace's unusual trapezoidal shape, with four sides of different lengths, reflects the limits set by the streets surrounding it. The smallest side of the four-storey building faces Piazza San Pantaleo, while its opposite, parallel but longer side faces Piazza Navona. Elements of the Braschi and Onesti insignias are numerous on the façade – in the Braschi family symbols of stars, and lilies withstanding a blowing wind, and in the Onesti symbols of lions'

Braschi, set on a field of giant repetitions of the word 'si'. The fascist slate – to which there was no alternative – won the election with nearly 99 per cent of the vote.

Mussolini's offices were at Palazzo Venezia, overlooking the Vittoriano monument. In order to isolate the monument and make it appear even more grand, he ordered the destruction of all the buildings abutting it. His propagandist nation-building campaign included the installation of the Tomb of the Unknown Soldier at Vittoriano, where it is now a key component of the monument. In May 1938, on the steps of the Vittoriano, Mussolini stood side-by-side with Adolf Hitler, who had been given a hero's welcome on his visit to Rome. Two years later, Italy would enter the the Second World War as Germany's ally.

heads with pine cones in their mouths. Architect Cosimo Morelli is responsible for the palazzo's design, including its façade, which looks to Renaissance and classical models. Its alternating rows of triangular and segmental pediments recall the façade of Palazzo Farnese, and its severe exterior suggests a new understanding or recognition of Roman residential architecture, where blocky, imposing facades gave way to open, airy interiors. The central, enclosed courtyard of Palazzo Braschi largely mimics the façade, except that it extends for only two floors – a third storey terrace looks down on the open courtyard.

Inside the palace, the focal point is a magnificent staircase designed by Morelli, very likely in collaboration with fellow architect Giuseppe Valadier, who also designed furnishings, decorative arts and silver tableware. With wide, shallow stairs spanning two storeys, the square staircase is supported by eighteen red granite columns, originally from a portico built by Emperor Caligula (ruled 37–41 CE), which are topped by Ionic capitals with the insignias of the Braschi and Onesti. The vaulted ceilings of the staircase are adorned with intricate plaster carvings, some of which, in typical Neoclassical manner, depict scenes from the Iliad and the Odyssey.

The numerous salons and rooms of the palace apartments are decorated in styles inspired by Pompeii and Herculaneum, with subject matter

Morelli-designed staircase at Palazzo Braschi. Lalupa/CC3.0

Oculus of the staircase at Palazzo Braschi.
Miguel Hermoso Cuesta/CC4.0

the artists either saw first-hand or in illustrations coming out of the excavations of those sites. Vaulted ceilings are painted with busy, vibrantly coloured scenes of grotesque figures and delicate patterns, while walls feature the trompe l'oeil architectonic effects, geometric motifs and scenes from classical mythology. Throughout the palace, ancient Greek and Roman sculptures sit side-by-side with their neoclassical counterparts, and murals and paintings depict both mythological scenes and the bucolic landscapes and heroic historical narratives popular in the Napoleonic era.

Despite the treatment of his uncle at the hands of the French, Papal nephew Luigi Onesti had motivation to adopt a taste for all things French. In the aftermath of Pius VI's death while a prisoner of France, Napoleon sought to reconcile with the Catholic church. Onesti, first ousted from Palazzo Braschi when the French claimed Rome, was reinstalled in 1809, when he was appointed Mayor of Rome, which was still under the control of France.

Onesti died in 1816, his palace – and Rome's last vestige of Papal shows of family wealth and supremacy – still unfinished. The palace was eventually sold to the Kingdom of Italy, which

Detail of a ceiling at Palazzo Braschi, depicting Apollo on a chariot. Livioandronico2013/CC4.0

had been established just ten years prior. From 1920 to 1943, Palazzo Braschi served as the headquarters of Benito Mussolini and the Partito Nazionale Fascista, or National Fascist Party. For years, the building was emblazoned with a giant relief sculpture of Mussolini's face. The palace fell into disrepair in the post-war years, until the 1950s, when it became the main location of the Museo di Roma (Museum of Rome). Today, the palazzo that stood witness to the most important decades in the formation of modern Italy serves as a fitting setting for the museum's collection of period costumes, vintage carriages, historical items and works of art from the Middle Ages through the nineteenth century.

HOW TO SEE IT: Palazzo Braschi sits on Piazza San Pantaleo, between the Corso Vittorio Emanuele II thoroughfare and Piazza Navona. There are entrances from both piazzas. Several bus lines run along Corso Vittorio Emanuele II (stop is S.A. Della Valle), and the 8 tram stops at Largo di Torre Argentina, a five minute walk from the museum. Opening hours are Tuesday to Sunday from 10 am to 7 pm, and admission is currently €9.50 for adults. For more information, visit **www.museodiroma.it/en.**

Il Vittoriano.

Vittorio Emanuele II Monument

The *Monumento Nazionale a Vittorio Emanuele* (Vittorio Emanuele National Monument), also known as the *Altare della Patria* (Altar of the Fatherland) and the *Vittoriano*, is an example of neoclassical architecture that can't be missed, quite literally. It's the largest national monument, not just in Rome, but in all of Italy, and typifies the grandeur and aggrandisement that were the hallmarks of Italy's neoclassical movement. The Vittoriano, as much as any other structure in Rome, symbolises the socio-political and propandising objectives in a work of architecture – concepts which Mussolini would refine to frightening effect just decades later.

The Risorgimento may be a short period in the long history of the Italian peninsula, but it's one of the most turbulent, unstable and formative periods in the modern history of Italy.

The stirrings of the Risorgimento (which literally translates to 're-rising' or 'rising again') began with the dissolution of the Holy Roman Empire in 1806 and Napoleon's final downfall at the Battle of Waterloo in 1815, which released Italy from French control. The regions of the Italian peninsula reverted to being governed as separate kingdoms, dukedoms and as the Papal States, which covered an irregularly shaped swath of central-northern Italy from Rome to Ravenna. But the seeds of unification had already been planted, and underground conversations around the concept of unification were occurring behind the walls of coffee houses and cafes throughout many of Italy's divided territories. By the mid-1800s, the kingdoms and dukedoms had begun the process of breaking with their foreign leaders; the most significant

King Vittorio Emanuele II ca. 1861.

break was the Sardinian revolution against Austrian rule, which culminated in 1859 with Austria's defeat.

The Sardinian King Vittorio Emanuele II now ruled over the combined Kingdom of Sardinia-Piedmonte – a unification of two of Italy's once independent and once Austrian-ruled states. Vittorio Emanuele battled Papal States' troops in Northern Italy and quickly annexed that portion of papal territories. Around this same time, General Giuseppe Garibaldi conquered Naples for Sardinia-Piedmont, meaning that apart from

Rome and parts of Lazio (the region surrounding Rome), which remained under the Papal States, Vittorio Emanuele controlled all of Italy. In 1861, the Kingdom of Italy was established, with Vittorio Emanuele II as its king.

The 1866 annexation of the Veneto, the region of Venice, to the Kingdom of Italy left only Rome outside of its control. In 1870, the Italian army marched into Rome and claimed the city, after then-Pope Pius IX refused an offer of a friendly hand over of the city to the Italian Kingdom. The Papal States, which had figured so dominantly in centuries of Italian history and politics, all but ceased to exist, and the Pope remained confined inside the Leonine Walls, the defensive enclosure around the Apostolic Palace and St Peter's.

Vittorio Emanuele II remained King of Italy until his death in 1878, though in his later years his governing role was greatly reduced and usurped by Italy's parliament. Still he is regarded as the 'Father of the Fatherland' – the figure most responsible for unifying Italy and establishing it as a central power in Europe. The Vittoriano monument, dedicated both to the king and to the decades-long struggle for unification, is imposing and powerful, intended to represent the potency – real and embellished – of the newly formed state.

The structure wasn't completed until 1935, but the design was finalised in 1885 by Giuseppe Sacconi, who won the role of lead architect in a design

The future site of the Vittoriano in 1870, prior to demolition.

competition but would not live to see its completion. Criticism of the monument began even before its construction, which required the complete demolition of a medieval neighbourhood, which included Roman ruins and several

historic churches. Construction also required carving into a huge section of the Capitoline Hill at a time when the area's archaeological layers and complexity were only beginning to be scientifically studied. The monument's grandiosity and its dominance of the Roman skyline were criticised, as were its lack of homogeny with surrounding

Il Vittoriano. Paolo Costa Baldi/CC3.0

Baroque and ancient structures. Architecturally, the monument has been criticised for being too cold, primarily due to its white marble construction and boxy, stacked design. Its obtrusiveness and unmistakable qualities have earned it several pejorative nicknames among Romans, ranging from 'the wedding cake' to 'the dentures' and 'the typewriter'.

Popular response to the Vittoriano notwithstanding, it remains an archetypal example of monumental neoclassicism, albeit minus the restraint of other contemporary buildings. Roman- and Greek-inspired elements define the façade, which includes Corinthian columns, carved acanthus leaves, friezes with relief sculptures, steps leading to a massive podium, an immense, heroic equestrian statue of Vittorio Emanuele II, and monumental allegorical sculptures. In borrowing the design principles of the great Classical empires, the Vittoriano was intended to be the first major symbol of the new collective Italian identity, and harken back to a time when Italy – by way of Rome – was the world's most powerful empire. The Kingdom of Italy was essentially a new-born nation building itself from scratch, and the Vittoriano monument was meant to convey its unity, strength and collective identity. Even in its nascent years, Italy was trying to position itself as a world power – including through disastrous invasions of North Africa – and the grandiose Vittoriano was always intended to be a

physical symbol of that megalomania.

The theme of unification is evident throughout the monument – it's not just the size and scale that represent the struggle to which it's dedicated. On either side of the monument are two small fountains representing the two seas surrounding Italy – the Adriatic to Italy's east and the Tyrrhenian to the west. Friezes along the oval-shaped base on which the Vittorio Emanuele II statue stands depict the regions of Italy personified, all of which are collectively supporting the new king. By

Sculptures depicting the regions of united Italy.
Carlomorino/CC4.0

Hard to miss anywhere in the city: Il Vittoriano as seen from Pincio Hill, 1 ½ mles away. Federampa/CC3.0

incorporating and acknowledging Italy's independent regions and geographical distinctions, yet depicting them in a partnership to (literally) support the new king, the Vittoriano acknowledges the localised identity of each region while nonetheless making it clear that the allied state has power above all.

Arguably, the monument has unified Italy, but perhaps not in the way Sacconi hoped. For many, it is a symbol of blind nationalism and cultural pretension rather than a site of civic tribute and pride as originally intended. (Its later associations with Mussolini and fascism only contributed to its controversial role in Italian identity.) For the most part, what unites Romans and Italians may be their universal distaste of the massive 'birthday cake' that dominates the city centre.

HOW TO SEE IT: Even if you're not intent on visiting the Vittoriano, you really can't miss it if you try. The massive white monument sits at Piazza Venezia and the bottom of Corso Cavour, the main north-south thoroughfare in central Rome. It's a point of reference for visitors, and the piazza in front is a major transit stop of city buses. The monument houses a museum dedicated to the Risorgimento, an art gallery (both free except during special exhibitions), the Altar of the Fatherland and the Tomb of the Unknown Soldier. Access to the monument is free, and a climb to the top offers sweeping views of the Roman Forum behind it. An elevator ride to the very top terrace – the only way to reach this area – costs €7. The monument is open daily from 9.30 am – 7.30 pm, with last admission at 6.45 pm. The closest Metro stop is Colosseo (Colosseum), and several buses, including 40, 44, 64 and 84, stop nearby. For more information, visit **http://www.turismoroma.it/cosa-fare/le-terrazze-del-vittoriano?lang=en**.

FASCISM & MUSSOLINI'S THIRD ROMAN EMPIRE

Foro Italico, Palazzo della Farnesina, Termini Station

The period of the Risorgimento is recalled with pride and nostalgia in Italy, when citizens of the newly formed country were united in their newfound identity and nationhood. But for most everyday Italians, particularly those living in the south, the end of the nineteenth and turn of the twentieth centuries offered little cause for optimism or national pride.

The new government overtly favoured Northern Italy over the south, in part because most elected and appointed officials were from the north, and in part because of lingering prejudices which regarded southern Italians as ignorant and backwards. The north industrialised and modernised, as Genoa became a centre for shipbuilding and military manufacturing, Turin, home of Fiat and Alfa-Romeo, grew a nascent automotive industry and Milan emerged as a banking capital.

Southern, and to a lesser extent, central Italy, continued to rely on agriculture to support its economy, often with calamitous results. Rural Italians in these regions essentially worked as tenant farmers, with no financial or housing security and often on the brink of starvation. Disease, hunger and crushing poverty drove millions of Italians from the south and Sicily to migrate, either to the north or to the United States. Meanwhile, the Kingdom of Italy was engaged in an aggressive and expensive policy of colonialism, which saw it invading and claiming as its territories Ethiopia, Libya, Somalia, Eritrea and parts of Greece.

Italy's entry into the First World War was widely unpopular among Italians.

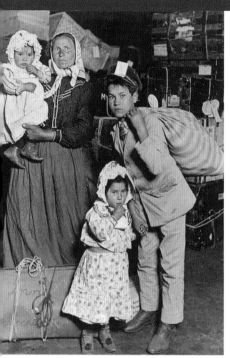

Italian immigrants arrive at Ellis Island, U.S. immigration station in New York Harbor.

Its army was unprepared and under-equipped to wage war, and while the Allies, of which Italy was a part, emerged victorious, the toll was profoundly felt. More than 650,000 soldiers and civilians were killed during the war, and a million more injured. The expected payoff in exchange for aligning with the Allies was to be the annexation of large parts of modern Croatia, the Tyrol region of Austria, plus Albania and the Greek Dodecanese Islands. Italy received only a portion of these territories after the war, and the 'mutilated victory' of these broken promises, plus the staggering debts run up in the country's failed

colonial ambitions, further fuelled popular discontent.

In the sixty years since its formation, Italy had had thirty-seven prime ministers, with most of them serving less than one year. Regional tensions were at an all-time high, agricultural and factory workers frequently staged strikes, and partisan violence, among forces representing anarchists, socialists, conservatives and nationalists, was the norm.

Into this crisis of leadership and amid the widespread, prolonged desperation of the Italian people walked Benito Mussolini – almost literally, with the promise to re-establish order, prop up the middle classes and restore Italy's status as a global power. A figure in Italian politics since 1919, his 1922 March on Rome – in which he didn't actually march, but arrived a day later – marked a decisive point in his quick rise to power. King Vittorio Emanuele III, grandson of Vittorio II, appointed

The March on Rome reaches Il Vittoriano, 1922.

1940 hand-coloured photo of Benito Mussolini by Roger Viollet.

Mussolini Prime Minister the next day. Within three years, Mussolini had dropped all pretence of constitutional government and positioned himself as dictator.

Mussolini's complicated legacy in Italy still resonates, more than seventy years after his execution by anti-fascists. He created an absolute police state in Italy, violently suppressed all political parties but his own, ordered the assassinations of his rivals, and led Italy in a disastrous wartime alliance with Adolf Hitler. He is also widely credited with pulling Italy out of the nineteenth century and into the modern era, with

ambitious and effective construction, transportation, and manufacturing programs that modernised the country, and created jobs, relative economic stability and ease of mobility.

Perhaps most surprising to modern visitors to Italy, and to Rome especially, is that so much evidence of Mussolini remains – in the distinctive form of Fascist architecture. From government offices to sporting facilities, train stations, planned cities and public squares, Mussolini's vision for the Third Roman Empire – the next great rising of Rome after the era of the Emperors and the Popes – remains most evident in his ambitious and grandiose plans for rebuilding the Eternal City.

Foro Italico (formerly the Foro Mussolini)

When work began on the Foro Mussolini in 1928, modernism as an aesthetic and philosophy was already entrenched in Europe. The style rejected what was perceived as the false pretence of neoclassicism, as well as neoclassicism's mimicking of the past. For a generation of artists, architects and intellectuals that had, during the Great War, witnessed the horrors of mechanised warfare, the decorative aspects of neoclassicism represented the outdated ideals of the now-irrelevant noble classes. For post-war Europe, reeling from years of conflict and searching for solutions to the challenges of modern life, neoclassicism was simply superfluous.

Fascist youth salute Mussolini, 1935.

In its place rose modernism, which championed the idea of 'form follows function' – that a building (or any industrial design) must first be completely functional and efficient. Architecturally, buildings were designed to improve lives, relieve overcrowding in cities and best serve the needs of the occupant. Decoration was minimal to non-existent, and used only to the extent that it complemented the object's function. Champions of the style in Germany included Walter Gropius and Mies Van der Rohe, and in France, Le Corbusier.

While modernism had different aesthetic proponents and offshoots across Europe and the United States, in Italy, its hybrid, and precursor to fascist architecture, was rationalism. Italian rationalism espoused the tenets of pure geometry and science in architectural design, and, like modernism, rejected anything deemed excessive or unnecessary. In fascist architecture, the simple geometry of rationalism met with the totalitarianism of Mussolini's state, for an architectural style that was minimalist, yet overwhelming in scale and referent to Rome's imperial past.

Mussolini's concept for a Third Empire drew on the ideals of Imperial Rome, and his sprawling Foro Mussolini (Forum of Mussolini) was an overt reference to the past glories of the Empire. Only Roman emperors had forums named after them, so in naming a new forum after himself, Mussolini's intentions were clear – to align himself and the state (and he was the state), with the illustrious empire of the past.

Casa delle Armi, an architectural anomaly in the Foro Mussolini

At the far southern end of the Foro Italico complex, behind an unsightly white fence sits one of the complex's most architecturally significant buildings, the former Casa delle Armi (House of Arms), which once housed the fascist fencing academy. Designed by Luigi Moretti – who would later design the famed Watergate complex in Washington, DC, the Casa delle Armi is an example of sleek, innovative modernism, minus the dogmatic style, heavy-handed symbolism, and severity of the surrounding fascist architecture. Currently used by CONI, the Italian Olympic Committee, this early work of Moretti appears to be in a poor state of repair and is marred by the ugly fence. Visitors can walk around the outside, but not enter.

The sprawling complex, located north of the centro storico and Vatican City, is today one of the clearest surviving examples of his totalitarian vision.

In Italy's youth, Mussolini saw the future of the Fascist party and of the new empire. In models borrowed both from classical Rome and from Adolf Hitler – with whom he was increasingly allied – Mussolini's fascism had at its epicentre the concepts of physical prowess, athletic perfection and mental sharpness in service to the state. In conjuring the idea of the strong young fascist willing to fight and die for his country – and his Duce – Mussolini imbued Italy's youth with nationalistic and imperialistic fervour. To that end, he ordered the construction of sports

Luigi Moretti's Casa delle Armi. 0000ff/CC3.0

The 1939 Ponte Duca d'Aosta bridge. antmoose/CC2.0

facilities throughout Italy. His 'city of sport' at the Foro Mussolini was the nation's largest training ground for the rising generation of young Italian men.

The forum would ultimately comprise two stadiums, an indoor pool, a tennis centre, a fencing academy and fascist party buildings, as well as vast open areas for assembly. Like its Ancient Roman prototypes, buildings were large and symmetrical. And much like the Colosseum – which fascist architects no doubt looked to for inspiration – they could hold large numbers of people, who could be assembled and dispersed quickly. A wide, new bridge across the Tiber, the Ponte Duca d'Aosta, opened

in 1939 and ensured that Romans could easily reach the Foro Mussolini. From the Papal Empire, fascist architects adopted the concept of the piazza or public square as a stage to which the public was drawn, overwhelmed and transfixed. Omnipresent and omnipotent in it all was Il Duce – his name, likeness, and slogans, along with the allegorical figures of fascism, appeared on every building, stadium, piazza, and statue.

But fascist style rejected key elements of both classical and papal architecture – most specifically their ornamentation and almost any trace of soft edges. The two buildings that frame the entrance to the Foro Mussolini, the

Academy of Physical Education, with the original fasces replaced by the Olympic logo.

former Academy of Physical Education to the right and the Centre for Political Preparation to the left, can be likened to stripped-down versions of a Roman basilica or a Renaissance palazzo. There's the mathematical Renaissance symmetry and repetition in rows of windows and matching wings, coupled with the scale and heroic sculpture of an ancient basilica.

Between the two buildings, Mussolini's answer to the victory columns and Egyptian obelisks of the Roman emperors still stands – a 60 ft tall, nearly 300 ton monolith carved of a solid block of Carrera marble, with the epigraph, 'Mussolini Duce' – Mussolini the Leader. Behind the monolith opens the Piazzale

dell'Impero, a large open square paved with black and white mosaics in the classical Roman style – except that these depict fascist allegories and symbols, as well as the 'Il Duce' and fascist slogans repeated across the piazza. At the end of the piazza, the Fountain of the Sphere centres around a 40 ton marble sphere, also from Carrera, said to represent the strength of fascism.

To the right of the fountain, the most overtly fascist component of the most overtly fascist complex in Italy is the Stadio dei Marmi – the Stadium of the Marbles. The stadium, one of two erected in a bid to bring the 1940 Olympic games to Rome, is ringed with fifty-nine – originally there were sixty – 12 ft tall statues of nude athletes, each representing a different sport

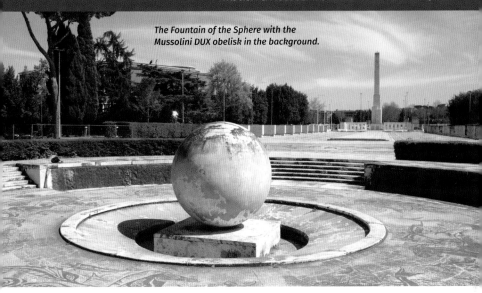

The Fountain of the Sphere with the Mussolini DUX obelisk in the background.

Statues at the Stadio dei Marmi, with the modern Olympic Stadium in the background.

and a different province of Italy. With their severe, angular features, looming presence and larger-than-life size, they are by modern standards nearly comical in their heroism and virility. For Mussolini and the crowds gathered to hear him speak or watch him as he watched a sports event, they were mighty sentinels, symbols of athleticism and strength of the Roman past and the Fascist present.

HOW TO SEE IT: The exterior complex of the Foro Italico, including the Stadio dei Marmi, the Piazzale dell'Impero and the Fountain of the Sphere are accessible to the public, though access to most interiors is limited. Foro Italico is north of central Rome and can be reached via Metro or bus. From Termini Station, the 910 bus terminates at the Foro Italico stop. From there, cross the Ponte Duca D'Aosta bridge to reach the Foro Italico. An alternative is to take the Metro A line to the Flaminio stop, then the 2 tram to the Mancini stop, then cross the bridge to the Foro. I recommend combining a visit to the Foro Italico with the Auditorium Parco della Musica and the MAXXI Museum (see Chapter 11). To do so, stop at the De Coubertin/Palazzetto Sport stop if on bus 910, or the Apollodoro tram stop if on tram 2. You can then continue on public transportation to the Foro, or make the twenty minute walk from MAXXI.

Palazzo della Farnesina (Palazzo del Littorio)

If the buildings and monuments of the Foro Mussolini document the development of fascist-style architecture, the building now known as the Palazzo della Farnesina represents the complete evolution of fascist design.

By the mid-1930s, the Kingdom of Italy, led by Mussolini and with King Vittorio Emanuele III as its figurehead, had expanded its colonial holdings and realised Il Duce's vision of a Third Roman Empire. Fascist party leaders felt that the new empire required a new architecture, something that sufficiently demonstrated the omnipotence of the new empire and referenced the models of classical Rome. They also sought a break with modernism – in part because it was an international style and in part because it had always been associated with socialism and communism – and fully represented the totalitarian ideals of fascism. The party also needed a new headquarters, to be built on a monumental scale that functionally could hold thousands of people and that symbolically demonstrated the might of the party and the empire.

Initial plans called for the new party seat to be named the Casa Littoria – for littore, or lictor, bearer of the fasces, the symbol of fascism – and located near the Colosseum, along the newly constructed Via dell'Empero (now Via dei Fori Imperiali). A design contest

Why are there still so many fascist buildings in Italy?

To most Italians and to most of the rest of the world, Italy's fascist period is regarded as a dark chapter in its history. Yet unlike Germany, where monuments and buildings built by and propagating the Nazi party were destroyed in the aftermath of the war, in Italy, especially in Rome, fascist architecture is everywhere. From government buildings to train stations to assembly halls, Mussolini's mark on the Eternal City is still felt, to the extent that some buildings still bear his name.

The answer to why so many of these paeans to fascism remain is multi-fold. First and foremost, Rome was not destroyed by wartime bombing. Though bombing raids, both by Allied and German planes, did heavily damage some areas and cause mass casualties, there simply wasn't the widespread destruction that occurred in other European cities. Second, fascist buildings were large, modern and functional – it didn't make sense to tear down transportation links and office buildings that were still necessary and useful to a country rebuilding itself after war. Thirdly, the aesthetic qualities of fascist architecture were valued in and of themselves, so there was an effort to preserve the buildings as part of the

'DUCE' mosaics remain at the Viale del Foro Italico, formerly the Piazzale dell'Impero.

historical record. Lastly – though far from the final word on the subject – post-war Italy's relationship with Mussolini has always been a difficult one, and the distinctive architectural style and modern infrastructure he brought to Italy are considered positive aspects of his legacy.

dragged on for several years, during which time there were disagreements about proper fascist style as well as where to build the new headquarters. Because of the challenges of constructing a huge new project in Rome's centre, the eventual Palazzo del Littorio was planned for a site adjacent to the Foro Mussolini, with the winning design by affirmed fascist architects Arnaldo Foschini, Vittorio Ballio Morpurgo, and Enrico Del Debbio.

Described as the 'most fascist of fascist buildings', the Palazzo del Littorio

Palazzo della Farnesina, the former Palazzo del Littorio.

overwhelms for its size alone – at 540,000 square metres it is one of the largest buildings in Italy. The palazzo's façade is 200 metres long and nearly 50 metres tall. The nine-storey structure contained 1,300 rooms, including two floors for Mussolini's offices. Its vast exhibition space was designed as the permanent home of the Exhibition of the Fascist Revolution, the propaganda-filled historical exhibit that more than 4 million Italians and foreigners had visited from 1932 to 1934. Plans called for a piazza in front – now a parking lot – ringed by arcades and capable of holding 600,000 people.

Like the great structures of the Roman Empire, the palazzo is clad in white

The Farnesina seen from the Stadio dei Marmi. 1012 Simone Ramella/CC2.0

travertine block, and its façade is severe and unyielding. Symmetrical rows of windows – particularly the two-storey-tall windows in what were Mussolini's offices – give the effect of authoritatively gazing down on human subjects below. The overall feel conveyed is one of imposing, impregnable strength.

Construction began on the Palazzo del Littorio in 1938 but was suspended in 1942, when the costs of the Second World War meant there were few resources for Mussolini's continued transformation of Rome. Construction was finished in the post-war years, largely according to the original design and with the same principal architects. Since 1959, the building has housed the Foreign Ministry of Italy, and is called Palazzo della Farnesina. It's named after the Farnese family – the same Farnese of Papal fame – who once owned the land on which it sits. So distinct is the building that the office of the Foreign Ministry is referred to as the 'Farnesina'.

HOW TO SEE IT: Palazzo della Farnesina is adjacent to the Foro Italico. The Farnesina's contemporary art collection is open to the public periodically and by reservation only. For information, see: **https:// collezionefarnesina.esteri.it**. To reach the Palazzo della Farnesina, follow the directions earlier in this chapter to the Foro Italico.

A side trip to EUR, Mussolini's city of the future

Visitors fascinated by fascist architecture should make a day trip to EUR, once the acronym for the Esposizione Universale Roma and now the standalone name of the suburban district south-west of central Rome. Construction of EUR began in the late 1930s, as the site was intended to host the World Expo of 1942, celebrate the

Palazzo della Civiltà, EUR. dalbera/CC2.0

twentieth anniversary of the March on Rome, and present a model city that touted the economic and cultural achievements of fascism. The expo was cancelled due to the Second World War, and Mussolini's city of the future wasn't completed until years after his death. But the designs of the original EUR were largely adhered to in the post-war years, with the result a severe, surreal landscape of government and private offices and headquarters. The 68 metre tall Palazzo della Civiltà Italiana (the Palace of Italian Civilisation) stands out among the sea of white travertine – and a surprising amount of green space. It's distinctive, forbidding design and massive dimensions have earned it the nickname 'the Square Colosseum'. It's now the world headquarters of Fendi fashion house, and is open for periodic art exhibits and special events.

To get to EUR, take the Metro B line in the direction of Laurentina, and exit at EUR Palasport or EUR Fermi.

Stazione Termini (Termini Station)

The gateway to Rome for hundreds of thousands of tourists and the transit hub for even more commuters, Termini Station – Stazione Termini – serves nearly 500,000 passengers daily. In Europe, it's second only to Paris' Gare du Nord ('Station of the North') in annual visitors. But unlike the Gare du Nord and the other Beaux-Arts railway stations across Paris, Termini straddles the lines between fascist architecture and the modern influences that followed. The building's phases were designed and executed under different political climates throughout decades of sporadic construction.

Construction began in 1937 when Mussolini ordered the demolition of the former station, which had been

Termini Station, with Piazza del Cinquecento in front.
Dasf Sturm / CC2.0

inaugurated in 1867 but soon proved to be of inadequate size. The new, larger venue was planned to coincide with the 1942 World Expo (see EUR sidebar, above), and was designed by Angiolo Mazzoni, a favoured architect of the Fascist Party and one of the chief influences in the development of the fascist aesthetic. Mazzoni's design featured two wings, where the majority of actual train and travel services would take place. His design called for a 12,000 square metre entrance hall clad in travertine block, and with no practical function other than to overwhelm visitors with its size and soaring ceiling.

When construction was suspended in 1943, only the two wings had been completed. Like the fascist buildings at EUR, the Foro Mussolini and elsewhere in Rome, they borrow heavily from Imperial Roman models – at Termini, the use of repeated rows of arches and

Termini Station, with the Mazzoni wing running along Via Giolitti, behind the post-war atrium and front hall.
Herb Neufeld/CC2.0

long, covered arcades were intended to pay homage to the nearby Baths of Diocletian and, just down the road, the Colosseum. The high walls and rows of uniform rectangular windows are hallmarks of fascist design.

After a design competition to complete the post-war station, building resumed in 1947 and the new station opened in 1950. The winning design, helmed by architects Eugenio Montuori and Annibale Vitellozzi, had the incongruent tasks of using Mazzoni's existing buildings and integrating them into a new design, yet clearly breaking from the repressive severity of fascist design. Their entrance atrium to the station is a graceful, glass-fronted structure in the form of a wavelike, flattened ribbed vault. The choice of an airy, organic, transparent design

was also a deliberate rejection of the monolithic, authoritarian aesthetics of fascism, and represents the post-war ideals of the free, democratic Republic of Italy. The frieze on the outside of the atrium is the 1950s work of artist and actor Amerigo Tot. Though his design has been praised for the way in which it captures the energy and movement of the trains, the choice of Tot was also symbolic – he had been a member of the Italian Resistance, or partisan movement, during the war.

A multi-story building, part of the post-war construction phase, is set behind the atrium, with a ticketing area on the first floor and offices and commercial space above. Its sleek modernist style connects both physically and aesthetically the old and new parts of the complex, and

The modernist atrium of Termini Station at its completion, 1950.

completes the transition from the cold rationalist of fascist design and the organic, dynamic tenets of post-war modernism. Mazzoni's wings are still there, integrated into the new design by a wide, covered gallery that runs the width of the station and connects the entrance and ticketing hall to the Mazzoni wings and a gallery area where trains arrive and depart.

The Montouri/Vitellozzi solution of a modern atrium is today diminished by the addition of shops and kiosks which extend into the reaches of the vaulted space and all but obliterate its form and sense of movement. Piazza del Cinquecento, the large bus transfer station in front of Termini, is abuzz with buses, taxis, hawkers, and suitcase-

Gallery connecting post-war sections to the Mazzoni wings. Kaz Ish/CC3.0

Termini Station at night. Ingolf/CC2.0

wielding tourists. The two side streets, along which Mazzoni's twin wings stretch, are clogged with traffic and garish storefronts. But seen from the right angle and with proper historical perspective, Termini Station remains a clear example of Italy's reconciliation of its fascist past and its post-war identity.

The Servian Wall

Outside Termini Station, to the left of the entrance atrium stands a segment of the Roman Servian Wall, which dates to as early as the sixth century BCE. The wall served as a defensive barrier for ancient Rome – stretching for nearly 7 miles, it was more than 12 ft wide and 30 ft tall. By the fourth or fifth century BCE Rome had already outgrown the confines of the Servian Wall, which was superseded by the third-century BCE Aurelian Walls. Though the Aurelian Walls are preserved in numerous places throughout the city, Termini Station provides one of the few places in Rome to see a complete section of the older Servian Wall.

HOW TO SEE IT: Chances are you'll pass through Termini Station at some point on your visit to Rome, so do take a moment to look around. The station faces Piazza del Cinquecento, and is wedged between Via Giovanni Giolitti and Via Marsala. Metro A and B lines both stop at Termini, as do dozens of bus lines. The station contains a subterranean and ground-floor shopping area, plus restaurants, bars and newsstands. Accessed from Via Giolitti or Mazzoni's southern/right-hand wing, Mercato Centrale is an excellent food hall for a variety of Roman-style street food.

CONTEMPORARY ARCHITECTURE IN ROME

Auditorium Parco della Musica, the Ara Pacis Museum & MAXXI Museum of 21st Century Arts

In the post-war years, Italy underwent a period of growth referred to as the 'Economic Miracle' – also called the 'boom economico' in Italian. The nation benefited from significant US aid, both in the form of immediate post-war assistance and then from the four-year Marshall Plan, intended to rebuild and modernise the infrastructure of war-shattered Europe.

From a country in ruins and a society which, pre-war, was already fractured between north and south, Italy built factories, highways and rail lines, and created a social safety net that improved the lives of Italians at every rung of the economic ladder. Upward mobility created by manufacturing jobs fomented a rising middle class.

Another prerogative of the Marshall Plan, apart from rebuilding Europe, was to create an economically strong, democratic buffer between Western Europe and the Iron Curtain, and Italy was seen as both critical to that agenda and vulnerable to communist influence. Thus even after the Marshall Plan ended, the US had incentive to continue to bolster Italy as a trade partner and close ally, and the boom continued well into the 1960s.

Poor and working-class Italians, many from the south, flooded into urban areas, where new social housing developments sprang up in city peripheries, which quickly became urbanised. Some of these projects stood out for their experimental approaches to densely packed housing, and many were designed by architects who had been

Modern apartment blocks near Ciampino, Rome.
Arpingstone/Public domain

buildings were built in neoclassical style or what might best be described as 'fascism-light' – with fascism's blocky rationalism and lack of ornament, minus its severe and jingoistic aspects.

Rome is described, often disparagingly, as a city that looks to its past rather than its future. Yet despite a struggling infrastructure, a sometimes dysfunctional city government and roads, bus fleets and monuments desperately in need of repair, there's a civic pride that comes from living in the city that once ruled over the largest empire in the world, and that is known for its enduring monuments and artistic treasures, which most visitors have seen in history texts or guidebooks long before they set foot in the Eternal City. Rome is Italy's most-visited tourist destination, and those millions of annual visitors pour into Rome not to see modern architecture, but for the glories of its past. Introducing a contemporary architectural aesthetic into this storied cityscape is fraught with complications. Perhaps that's why it didn't occur in earnest until the turn of the twenty-first century, with the debut of three innovative and controversial projects in or near the historic centre.

favourites of the Fascist Party. Still more were blocky, banal apartment buildings that have not aged well on Italy's cityscapes and ultimately contributed to a sense of urban blight outside city centres.

Meanwhile, the architecture of Italy's city centres, especially in non-industrialised cities like Rome, which did not incur major damage from Allied or German bombs, remained largely static. Most of Rome's centre within the Aurelian Walls was, and is still, the Rome of Mussolini, of the neo-classicists, of the Baroque era and of the Roman emperors. From approximately 1950, when the last of the fascist-era building projects were completed with a post-war political scrubbing, to the 2000s, no contemporary building projects were undertaken in the historic centre. Even in the San Lorenzo district, where proximity to a major railyard meant extensive wartime bombing, post-war

Auditorium Parco della Musica

Founded in 1585, the acclaimed Accademia Nazionale di Santa Cecilia music academy has counted as members and honorary members renowned musicians and composers, including

Entrance to Parco della Musica.

Corelli, Rossini, Mendelssohn and Mahler. From 1908 to 1936, its resident concert hall was the Augusteo, a 3,000-seat auditorium built into the ruins of the first-century BCE Mausoleum of Augustus. The drum-shaped tomb, nearly 300 ft in diameter and once nearly 140 ft tall, held the sarcophagi and funerary urns of Emperor Augustus, his wife, Livia, several subsequent emperors and dozens of imperial family members. After the 410CE Sack of Rome by the Visigoths, the mausoleum was used at various times as a fortress, a garden, and a bullfighting ring before being converted into a concert hall. In 1936, as part of his revitalisation of Rome, Mussolini ordered the demolition of the Augusteo auditorium,

restoration of the mausoleum and the reconstruction of the square blocks around the mausoleum. That left the Accademia Nazionale di Santa Cecilia without a permanent concert hall for the rest of the twentieth century.

When architect Renzo Piano and his firm won the design contest to create a permanent residence for the academy, he was already – and remains – Italy's best-known living architect, having burst onto the international stage with his co-design of the revolutionary Centre Georges Pompidou in Paris, which opened in 1977. Piano's subsequent major works have included airport terminals, museums and cultural centres, and skyscrapers, including London's iconic The Shard. His 1994 winning design would be located in the Flaminio neighbourhood just north of the historic centre, at the site of the 1960 Olympic Village and Flaminio Stadium, which had served as an Olympic venue. The location outside of, but connected to, the city centre was chosen firstly due to logistics – there simply wasn't available open space within the centre to build a complex of any size. The second motivation was to bring an artistic and cultural meeting place to the close-in Roman suburbs: the Olympic complex had quickly fallen out of use after the 1960 games, and the surrounding neighbourhood was in need of revitalisation.

The finished complex that makes up the Auditorium Parco Della Musica consists of three indoor concert halls, an outdoor amphitheatre, a theatre, gardens and meeting spaces, for a total seated capacity of approximately 7,500 guests. The complex is remarkable, not just for its contemporary design, but also in its execution of modern architectural principles, specifically, the idea that architecture is about more than materials and physical forms.

Like Piano's other projects, the complex is stunningly out-of-the-ordinary, with three pod-like, oblong domes – which Piano calls 'music boxes' as its focal point. Clad with lead panels, the domes reflect light differently throughout the day, effectively changing the colour and appearance of the building depending on the time and

season. Where the roof meets the sides of each dome – affectionately and not-so-affectionately referred to as 'beetles' or 'blobs' by critics – a gentle wave-like formation seems to overtake the sides of the structure, fold in and bend to the roof. The domes appear to float above the ground – an effect also aided by

Construction delays

Building projects in Rome very often run into delays, since it's hard to put a shovel in the ground of the Eternal City without hitting ancient ruins. Parco della Musica was no exception. Soon after construction began in 1995, workers discovered the ruins of a Roman villa complex dating to the early sixth century BCE. Piano had to make major revisions to the design in order to incorporate the ruins and add a small museum to artefacts recovered from the site. Completion of the complex was delayed by one year – or just the blink of an eye in Rome's 3,000-year history.

Roman villa remains at the Parco site.

The Cavea outdoor amphitheatre at Parco della Musica.

One of three dome-shaped auditoriums at the Parco.

Detail of the domes.
giorgio minga/CC3.0

Interior, Sala Santa Cecilia, Parco della Musica.
Maria Oik/CC2.0

the placement of the Cavea, the sunken outdoor amphitheatre, a decision intentionally made to emphasise the shape and size of the dome. Further, the domes suggest the familiar domes landmarks of Rome, the bodies of musical instruments, and the organic, flowing qualities of music.

Connected by a main hall, the interiors of the theatres are each distinct. The Sala Petrassi hall, the smallest of the three, is a versatile, flat-floored performance hall, designed to host events ranging from music to dance and theatre. The next largest space is the Sala Sinopoli, with a modular design and flexibility on arranging and staging. The largest and most lavish of the three halls is the Santa Cecilia Hall, designed

with undulating American cherry wood walls and ceiling panels, chosen to enhance the acoustics, resonate with the music and suggest the colour and materials of classical instruments. All halls feature dark woods and rich colours, inspired by the string instruments played within. In homage to Rome's ancient monuments, travertine floors and terracotta bricks are used throughout.

Parco della Musica was conceived as an urban, multiuse centre for the arts and recreation, with gardens, grassy lawns and a playground in addition to its open-air and enclosed concert facilities, and it remains Rome's most

Albarubescens/CC4.0

HOW TO SEE IT: The grounds and Cavea amphitheatre of Parco della Musica are open to the public during daytime hours, and the indoor concert halls are sometimes accessible outside of performance times. It's also possible to walk around the perimeter of all the domes and appreciate their scale and design. There are three museums on-site, including two devoted to archaeology and another of classical musical instruments. Design-focused guided tours of the complex are available in English, currently on weekends. There is also a bar, a restaurant and a gift shop. Visit **https://en.auditorium.com/** for more information.

To reach Parco della Musica, take the 910 bus from Termini Station to the Parco Rimembranza stop, then walk west about five minutes. The 223 bus from Termini stops at Pilsudski, a one minute walk from the complex. Or take Metro line B to Flaminio. From Flaminio, take the 2 tram to the Ankara/Tiziano stop, and walk ten minutes east to the complex. See Chapter 9 for suggestions on combining a visit to MAXXI and the Foro Italico.

important venue for the performing arts. His innovative project marked a great step into the present for the architecture and aesthetics of Rome, and set the contemporary precedent for projects that would follow.

Museum of the Ara Pacis

Mussolini's interest in the Mausoleum of Augustus and the area surrounding it was not limited to the mausoleum itself. He envisioned himself as the Augustus of modern Italy, and his plan, of building a Third Empire and restoring order and prestige to Rome and the rest of Italy, was modelled on Augustus' 'Pax Romana' – the Roman Peace that was ushered in at the beginning of Augustus' reign as the first Emperor of Rome. (That peace was relative, of course, as Rome, while stable at home, was constantly expanding its empire through forced colonisation and armed conquest, also the model that Mussolini favoured.)

In the area bordering the Mausoleum of Augustus, Il Duce envisioned a grand square, to be named Piazza Augusto Imperatore, that would affirm the Third Empire of fascism as the preordained successor to the First Empire of Augustus. The restoration and 'liberation' of the Mausoleum of Augustus, which included the demolition of the buildings nestled next to the round tomb, was one phase of the refashioning of the area. On three sides of the newly isolated mausoleum, stern government buildings went up,

The Ara Pacis, or Altar of Peace, in its present location. Ben Demey/CC2.0

their facades decorated with motifs that freely blended fascist, Christian and Roman/Latin iconography and inscriptions.

The fascist-era Ara Pacis pavilion, photographed in 1970. Indeciso42/CC4.0

Closest to the Tiber, on the west side of the piazza, a new glass pavilion housed the Ara Pacis, or Altar of Peace. Inaugurated in 9 BCE on a site several hundred metres from the mausoleum, the carved, marble altar to the Pax Romana lay buried under metres of silt from the Tiber floodplain and later, under a palazzo built over it. The altar came to light during renovations of the palazzo in the 1900s, and in the 1930s, Mussolini ordered its excavation and transfer to Piazza Augusto Imperatore.

The pavilion that first housed the Ara Pacis at its current location was, by the close of the Second World War, in poor condition, and this was not remedied in the ensuing decades. Heat, humidity and water infiltrations caused ongoing damage to the nearly 2,000-year-old

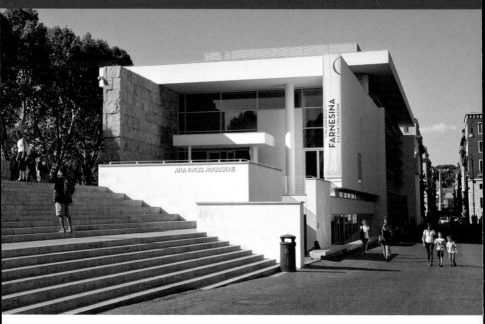

The Meier-designed Museo dell'Ara Pacis.
FaceMePLS/CC2.0

altar, but a permanent remedy wasn't seriously considered until the 1990s.

American architect Richard Meier,

Museum façade from Piazza Augusto Imperatore.

like his contemporary Renzo Piano, had already achieved 'starchitect' status by the time he was selected to design the new Museo dell'Ara Pacis to replace the fascist-era pavilion. Meier's design stoked controversy before the first stone was set, in part because he was chosen by Rome's then-mayor, thus bypassing a design competition like those typically held for important new city projects. Meier's project was also faulted for its starkly contemporary design, which critics – including nearby residents – claimed was completely out of context with Rome's historic centre. Yet Meier took inspiration from the ancient city – and even from the fascist facades nearby – and reinterpreted it for modern application. Columns, albeit sleek, unadorned ones – are used to

Fountain and stairs at the approach to the museum.

The Ara Pacis seen from the western side, with trees along the River Tiber embankment reflected in the museum windows. Lalupa/CC4.0

support the roofing structure both inside and out. Rough-hewn travertine block is used for some exterior walls, echoing both the colour and material of the fascist buildings on the piazza and the Roman remains across the city. A shallow, rectilinear fountain gives way to low, wide steps that lead to the museum entrance and offer

a processional effect, suggestive of how ancient worshippers might have approached the altar to worship and leave offerings.

Though travertine is used throughout the museum, its main materials are glass and concrete. The large cube room that houses the Ara Pacis is almost entirely glass, with large skylights that shine natural light on the ancient structure. The objective – which some say Meier actually failed to

Architect Richard Meier's signature on the plaza in front of the museum.

achieve – is for emphasis to be on the temple itself, rather than the structure protecting it. Though the space is heavy on glass, it aims to control light by way of thin horizontal supports across the glass curtain wall, which help both to support the structure and break up the strong light. The insulated glass windows are treated with a curtain of air, which prevents condensation and creates an internal microclimate to protect the marble altar, which sits on a raised platform in the centre of the building. Unlike most museums whose collections are visible only upon entering, the glass curtain walls, particularly the one on the Tiber/west side of the museum, allows passers-by to observe the altar at all hours of the day.

The museum opened in 2006 to both fanfare and disdain – perhaps more of the latter than the former. While advocates praised the building's smart use of light and focalisation on the Ara Pacis rather than on the building itself, critics called it overbearing and insensitive to its historical surroundings. An editorial in the *New York Times* described the new museum as 'absurdly overscale' and indifferent to the antique beauty of Rome. After being elected to office in 2008, Rome's mayor Gianni Alemanno vowed to tear down the Meier building and launch a new design competition for its replacement. Alemanno is gone, but the Museo dell'Ara Pacis remains, one of the most controversial – and discussion-worthy – structures in Rome.

HOW TO SEE IT: The Museo dell'Ara Pacis is located at Lungotevere in Augusta, a ten minute walk from the Spanish Steps and the Spagna Metro stop (line A). Several bus lines stop at or near Piazza Augusto Imperatore, including the 70, 81, 87, 492 and 628 lines. Current opening hours are daily from 9.30 am to 7.30, with last admission one hour before closing. Admission is €10,50 for adults, or €15 including entrance to special exhibits. Visit **http://www.arapacis.it/en** for more information.

MAXXI exterior.

MAXXI (Museo nazionale delle arti del XXI secolo/National Museum of 21st Century Arts)

Construction on Renzo Piano's Parco della Musica was already well underway in 1998, when Rome's Minister of Culture announced a design competition to build nearby Rome's first cultural complex dedicated to art of the twenty-first century. The competition was awarded to architect Zaha Hadid, who had already stirred waves for her gravity-defying designs and treatment of buildings as works of sculpture. Hadid's design for what would become the Museo nazionale delle arti del XXI secolo/National Museum of 21st Century Arts – fortunately called MAXXI for short – is an example of her career-defining aesthetic concepts – graceful, massive, yet seemingly weightless

Under the exterior portico, MAXXI.

forms that fold and curve in space. Like Parco della Musica, the MAXXI complex is in Flaminio, built on the site of an abandoned military barracks. Together with Piano's Parco, Hadid's MAXXI newly defined the Flaminio precinct as Rome's hub for cutting-edge, contemporary art and architecture.

MAXXI is divided into two separate museums, devoted to art and architecture respectively and totalling more than 20,000 square metres. Inside and out, MAXXI is the antithesis of the architectural past of Rome. Gone are the geometrically balanced and city-block

Cantilever level with windows.

wide dimensions of Rome's ancient, Renaissance and fascist edifices, replaced by curves and angles which intersect each other without apparent

Zaha Hadid in 2013. Dmitry Ternovoy/Free Art License

The Legacy of Zaha Hadid

In the 1980s, when Iraqi-born Zaha Hadid was a newly minted architect in London, her designs were considered too radical to actually be built. Her first major commission didn't occur until 1991, after which her creative career caught fire. For decades, she was one of the most sought-after architects in the world, especially when a project was to be realised in a way that would be daring, breath-taking and outlandishly contemporary. She won architecture's most prestigious prizes and was made a Dame by Queen Elizabeth II. Hadid died in 2016 at the age of 65, unexpectedly and after a short illness. Posthumous accolades regularly refer to her as the world's great female architect, but qualifying her achievements based on her gender gives short shrift to her rightful title as one of the greatest visionaries of the twenty-first century.

reason, and corridors and staircases that defy gravity and pierce the façade from within.

MAXXI's exterior, surrounded by a large pedestrian plaza, is flowing, surprising and incredibly complex. The main entrance to the building is through glass-doors, part of a glass wall set under a heavy portico formed by the second floor, which extends over the entry and is supported by rows of steel columns, creating a modern colonnade. Above that, another floor is set back, and emerged perpendicularly, with a large rectangular section cantilevering out over the building's plaza. Mirrored glass windows at the end of the cantilever reflect the piazza and neighbouring buildings, providing an urban example of contextualism, the contemporary principle of designing buildings sympathetic to their environments.

From an aerial view, the MAXXI museum forms what can best be described as a reclining L shape, effectively creating two large wings connected by a central atrium. Walkways – often visible as small rectangles protruding from the exterior – gently weave through the centre of the museums, creating a natural flow of traffic for visitors.

Inside the museum, the stairs and walkways cross over each other above the atrium, creating what creatively could be called a knot to tie the two wings and three floors together. Modern,

MAXXI interior with installation.

MAXXI interior. Commonurbock23/CC3.0

industrial-inspired materials like cement and steel are the primary construction mediums, creating a contemporary and neutral palette as the backdrop for the art displayed within.

Throughout the museums, the seemingly random intersections continue, though they're designed in such a way as to encourage the flow of humans through the space. Large, open spaces serve as both flexible exhibition spaces and communal meeting spaces. Though the windows and forms of the building may look random and, indeed, even a little brutalist from the exterior, it's clear from the atrium that allowing natural light to enter the space was a central factor in planning the project.

This fits right in line with key principles of contemporary architecture: using the site's orientation to direct and control light, and prioritising functionality in design decisions. Other notable design details include the gently curved staircases that intersect the building, literally and metaphorically blending art and architecture, the two wings of the museum.

After more than ten years of planning and construction, MAXXI opened in 2010, and was immediately hailed as a triumph for Hadid and for Rome. Hadid's work at MAXXI and even more so her future projects, including the Galaxy SOHO complex in Beijing and the Heydar Aliyev Center in Baku, Azerbaijan, demonstrates her interpretation of deconstructivism, the post-modern concept that buildings should appear to be arbitrarily attached fragments, rather than cohesive and unified spaces. Deconstructivism was a concept developed in response to the clean, simple lines of modernism and postmodernism that swept the European architectural scene in the mid- to late twentieth century. Though there are sharp angles at MAXXI, it would be difficult to find one that is ninety degrees – curvature is the defining characteristic of this remarkable complex.

HOW TO SEE IT: MAXXI is located on Via Guido Reni, west of Via Flaminia in the Flaminio neighbourhood. Current opening hours are Tuesday to Friday/Sunday from 11 am to 7 pm, and Saturdays to 10 pm. The museum is closed on Monday. Admission is €12 for adults. Visit www.maxxi.art/en for more information. To reach MAXXI from central Rome, take the 910 bus from Termini, or Metro line A to Flaminio, then tram 2 to the Apollodoro stop. I recommend combining a visit to MAXXI with the Auditorium Parco della Musica and the Foro Italico (see Chapter 11). To do so, take the 910 bus to the De Coubertin/Palazzetto Sport stop, or tram 2 to the Apollodoro stop. After touring the Parco della Musica, visit MAXXI, then continue on public transportation to the Foro, or make the twenty minute walk from MAXXI.

INDEX